WHEN LIFE SENDS YOU LEMONS, MAKE LENNONAID

WHAT JOHN LENNON'S LIFE DID FOR MINE

KAYA JOHN

BALBOA PRESS
A DIVISION OF HAY HOUSE

Balboa Press books may be ordered through booksellers or by contacting:

Balboa Press
A Division of Hay House
1663 Liberty Drive
Bloomington, IN 47403
www.balboapress.com
1 (877) 407-4847

Because of the dynamic nature of the Internet, any web addresses or
links contained in this book may have changed since publication and
may no longer be valid. The views expressed in this work are solely those
of the author and do not necessarily reflect the views of the publisher,
and the publisher hereby disclaims any responsibility for them.

The author of this book does not dispense medical advice or prescribe the use
of any technique as a form of treatment for physical, emotional, or medical
problems without the advice of a physician, either directly or indirectly. The
intent of the author is only to offer information of a general nature to help
you in your quest for emotional and spiritual well-being. In the event you use
any of the information in this book for yourself, which is your constitutional
right, the author and the publisher assume no responsibility for your actions.

Any people depicted in stock imagery provided by Thinkstock are models,
and such images are being used for illustrative purposes only.
Certain stock imagery © Thinkstock.

Print information available on the last page.

ISBN: 978-1-5043-8942-6 (sc)
ISBN: 978-1-5043-8944-0 (hc)
ISBN: 978-1-5043-8943-3 (e)

Library of Congress Control Number: 2017915295

Balboa Press rev. date: 10/25/2017

CONTENTS

ACKNOWLEDGEMENTS

Thank you Jean Quinn for telling me I had a book in me.

Thank you Pam Eelman for resurrecting the writing and helping me with my personal history.

Thank you Sara Beth Force for the reverence and respect you gave me and my writing and your depth of understanding.

Thank you Martha Freeman for the gift of your time, exquisite editing and support with my writing.

Thank you my dear husband Rob for unwavering belief in me, my capabilities and the story.

Thank you Karen McGlynn for your encouragement and involvement in my writing and for your chiropractic skills as well as your staff for keeping my body going for many years.

Thank you Shirley Pitcairn for your love, friendship, and willingness to listen to my progress on the writing over many intimate sharing and delightful luncheons.

Thank you Jacqueline Summers for helping me save my life so many years ago. You are an extraordinary person, writer and therapist.

Thank you: Delsie, Renee, Christine, Sherry, Janet, Marie, Stephanie, Andi, Don Swain, Ruth, Judy, Susan, Marianne, Joyce, Cindy, Sarah, Maureen & Franco, and Shey.

Overcoming a difficult childhood and beginning
a spiritual journey through the music of the
Beatles and John Lennon as a solo artist

This book is dedicated to Sid Bernstein, bringer of the
Beatles and the British Invasion of 1964, a kind hearted man
of peace who spent his life encouraging artists and everyone.

DREAM OF JOHN & YOKO

Dream: (while sleeping at night) Yoko and I are standing beside a car that has John Lennon sitting in the driver's seat. He is saddened, feeling the world did not receive his message as deeply as he intended. He feels he has failed. All that he did and said and people still don't get it. What can be done? Slowly, a large tear falls from each of his eyes. I turn towards Yoko and ask if I can wipe John's tears away. She gives me permission. I lean in and am deeply struck by how close I am to this man's face, the man who I so admire and feel so grateful to; I can see the texture of his skin, the pores on his familiar face. I take my hand and I wipe the tears away. I awake. I feel the dreams truth and realness. I lay calm, feeling emotion flow through my body. It is time to get writing.

MEDIUM TRANSCRIPT (PSYCHIC MEDIUM DEBORAH REES CHANNELED INTERACTION BETWEEN MY FATHER AND ME TEN YEARS AFTER HIS PASSING)

Deb: "One of the first things I get is even though you are very softly spoken, composed and together; you've had SUCH a life. Can you understand that? This totally belies the way you appear. You appear like you would have had a nice upbringing – that everything was calm, that everything was wonderful and I don't get that from you. Can you understand that Dad is passed over? I'm going to bring him in first. As soon as I said the name Dad, I got loads of emotion from him. He gives me the feeling there is loads of history between you. It's not just father and daughter. He gives me the feeling of regret (from Dad). I feel as if you were a very shy little girl is what he tells me – you were shy and introverted and I also feel that sometimes you would have been nervous of dad. I want you to know that as he comes in here, he feels very humbled to me. I feel in life he would have been like a bull, can you understand that he gives me the words raging bull. It's important (and he makes me cry) that he comes in humbly for you – so that you know where he is right now – I got a lovely feel to him – I feel he says to you: 'your heart is so pure and so sweet.' The feeling that he gives me is that despite everything you didn't become hard, you didn't turn callous – can you understand this could have caused you to have easily turned to stone."

It is because of the Beatles that I did not turn to stone.

BEATLE BLISS

You have to understand Beatle Bliss. I just listened to *If I Needed Someone* and let the melody lift me up and up, my body swaying, my foot tapping till ecstasy was reached. Sensations in the back of the throat, tears in my eyes, my body sweating, joy and happiness, feeling good, bliss. The Yogis get there – I open myself to Beatle music, I'm there.

BEGINNING

I have retraced the first time I heard the Beatles music to about twelve forty in the afternoon, January 25, 1964. I was eleven years old.

I grew up in the suburbs of Philadelphia, original home of the television show, American Bandstand with Dick Clark. I watched it faithfully and sang and danced to the music in my living room. One week a tune I heard on Bandstand was playing over and over again inside my head. I excitedly waited to find out what song this was and the name of the band. The show had a large chart for the top ten songs of the week. They would slide a board away to reveal the titles one at a time from ten to one. At number two I heard the song that was in my head, *She Loves You* by The Beatles. Then I found out they had another song at number one, *I Want to Hold Your Hand*.

We had a local music shop that had a record player so you could hear the music you were considering buying. The owner would order me obscure songs I had heard on the hit or miss segment of Bandstand. But these Beatle records were easy to get. I still remember as we got back into the car my Dad said: "Well, if this is all it takes to make my little girl happy, I'll buy her Beatle records." I believe a lot happened in this moment, some association. I had a tragic start in life with my father experiencing violent sexual abuse as a young child. In adolescence I received next to no attention from him and what little I got was receding quickly as I got older. Somehow I heard from him that I would receive happiness in this way.

This is a form of love that is available from my father through this music. I remember my father's reaction to the new sound. My father loved big band music and had a good singing voice. He could distinguish high quality and instantly heard it in the Beatles music. He immediately heard the talent in George's guitar playing and would often have me play *Can't Buy Me Love* so he could hear the guitar lick in the instrumental break. My father was moved to tears years later when I played *Yesterday* on the piano for him for his birthday.

That first day I returned home with my two forty-fives, I had my first picture of the Beatles. Looking back, I feel the significance of that moment: the wonder of it, my first glimpse of these universal friends who would orchestrate the events of my growing up.

Years later I realized I saw an Asian touch to John face, which would certainly be significant for him later in his life. I did not pick him as my favorite that day. I chose Paul. He was the cutest, though I didn't find any of them exceptionally attractive. It really wasn't the best picture. Their hair was actually quite short by later standards and George and Ringo still had some of the gawkiness of youth.

My next memory takes me to the first Ed Sullivan appearance. On the big night, my parents and I watched from our living room with my newly arrived kittens, a gift for my eleventh birthday.

As the Beatles began to perform, I quickly found Paul and within thirty seconds decided against him. He was too cute. He seemed conceited and contrived.

I decided I'd better take another look. Then it happened. Yes, a cosmic flash of white light and a momentary awareness of all that would come to pass and it felt like lightning. When I looked around the room, nothing had changed. My parents were simply watching. Nothing had happened to them. But for me, my heart and soul was now riveted to that man out front with the "cocky, sexy, spread-eagle stance."* John Lennon was the most empowered human being I had ever seen. He was the source. He was a powerhouse of psychic energy and physical presence. For now and forever, all my life through, in all I do, it would be John.

Within moments of this experience their names were flashed above them and under John's name were written "sorry, girls, he's married." I remember thinking it figures. Sadly, by sixth grade I was already affirming that what I wanted was unattainable.

But don't think I didn't vow to get to him and don't think I didn't. Few people could have had less opinion of their own worth than I did or felt less capable of creating their own life back then. But somehow I set course and over the distance of miles, years and social strata I did touch base with Lennon's life. He was dead five years and even though that made it a bit anticlimactic it was not without its rewards and pleasure. Years later I would remember fondly and with gratitude the brief moments I had in his home and with his family.

I remember a day soon after they became popular when I used to spend my days on the couch ill with chronic bronchitis, a stack of Beatle magazines at my side. One day as I was holding

---

* Nicholas Schaffner, The Beatles Forever, Cameron House 1977

them, I said a prayer. I already was aware that popular music styles came and went but asked God for the Beatles to please never go away. I think back on this when I am hearing the Beatles on the radio, attending Beatle conventions and sharing their music with each new generation. I really felt touched by the ad for the book by Nicholas Schaffner: "In 1964, they were just another pop group, now they are The Beatles Forever."

Before I go into detail about the Beatles I want to give you an idea of what the Beatles helped me to survive. I credit the Beatles from keeping me from despair. The joyful energy I found in their music and the message in their lyrics took me on a journey from a life of sadness and pain to a life filled with love, friendship and wonderful experiences. They transformed my world view from negative to positive and began my spiritual awakening. They were my vehicle from darkness to light.

MY BIRTH

Full Moon

No one was looking forward to my being born, perhaps least of all me. It was 1952, the height of American moral propriety at least on the surface. My mother, already divorced with a son ten years old became pregnant with me. My father was in what he called a forced marriage to a woman who was pregnant with a child my father sometimes claimed as his. They were living with his mother who controlled the family's substantial wealth; she was the one who had it. My father was used to it. He hadn't really totally figured out how to make enough on his own without her supplementing.

My father said my mother was the love of his life but yet he never figured out how to treat her with kindness and respect. Part of the tragedy of my growing up was that the love between us all was palpable but overshadowed by anger, violence, pain and insanity.

The love of my mother's life was a married millionaire, twenty years her senior from New York City. He made his money selling chicken on the streets of Manhattan. They met through a mutual friend while my mother's first husband was in the service in World War II. They would rendezvous at a swank hotel when he came to her town on business. After my mother died I found a letter she had written to God begging for forgiveness for her having lost her way. During a long interlude between visits my mother's life changed forever.

My mother met my father through her sister. My mother's sister convinced my mother to go out with my father as a thank you for a huge personal favor he had done for her. He mentioned how attractive he found my mother. She grew up being overweight and matronly with a pixie haircut her mother forced on her but then did an ugly duckling turn around the summer of her 9th grade. The pictures of my mother in her twenties and thirties before she spent prolonged time with my father enthrall me. She is the most beautiful woman I have ever seen. And I'll tell you why. Oh yes, she is physically beautiful but it's the feeling of her: a feminine combination of softness, strength, intelligence and love streaming from her eyes. This is the essence of femininity for me. I want to know this person. I want to be with this woman. I want "her" to be my mother.

My father wanted an abortion, my mother did not. My mother attempted an abortion at my father's insistence but I survived it. I survived by hanging on really tight. Unfortunately this became a life pattern, I often held onto people and situations too tightly and too long when it would have served me better to let go. I had a friend who had a dog grooming salon. I was with her one day and saw a cute Sheltie dog just standing in the room, shaking. I asked her why. She told me there had been an attempt as a puppy to get rid of it by flushing it down the toilet but it had survived. Unfortunately, it was eight years later and the dog was still shaking, I feel like that dog.

Reliving the experience year's later in therapy I kept repeating "Ten, twenty-seven, fifty-two, I'm coming through!" Asked why I hung on so tight, I answered: "I have to be here for The Beatles! It's why I'm coming here! For all the joy and fun and positive changes they will make! I'm going to be part of this,

I'm not going to miss this, and I'm going to be here! I'm part of John Lennon's team!"

Mom later told me she felt I was Jesus and her's baby. She believed he protected me and helped her keep me until I was birthed.

So then the millionaire tells my mom that he will divorce his wife and marry her but her mother tells her she should marry the father of the child. Wow, for me, that's a feminist debate issue right there. Was that what was best for my mother and me? Who has the authority here? Who has the power? My mother was still regretting the choice when I was an adolescent and would periodically approach me with the brainstorm of the two of us going on a crash diet which included rolling back and forth on the living room floor to get the weight off our hips. When we lost some weight she was going to call her old lover and he would come and get us and she would tell me how I would be really loved and rich, not poor and treated with disdain at best. She never called but I would believe her every time and wait for his to happen.

So what did happen is my father divorced his present wife and my parents married and his money was withdrawn. My father's mother disowned him completely until twenty years later when my mother called her and told her she thought she should know her son was very ill. He had totally collapsed from Multiple Sclerosis. My mother was scarred from her neck to her waist from the shingles she had while she carried me. She disguised her pregnancy by not eating. When she went to the hospital to deliver, they told her to go home; she couldn't be any more than a little over four months pregnant. Do I have food issues? I was born in the charity ward of a hospital, on the biggest and brightest full moon my father told me he had ever seen. I was born a little over five pounds but then went down to five pounds when my mother attempted to nurse me. Her milk had turned bad from her stress and poisoned me. While nursing me she noticed I was getting sick so she squeezed her nipple and the color of her milk was green. I almost died again.

I recently read a book on the Beatles where it mentions that when Lennon's first wife Cynthia was home heavily pregnant with Julian, John was seen sitting at the bars making out with his girlfriend. My mother was like that girlfriend. My mom played that same role in my father's life. What if John had gotten the other woman pregnant too? I can easily see the connection between John and my father. But the extremely significant difference between the two and the stepping off point for me and John was Lennon's lifelong work to transform himself into a better person, something that never occurred to my father.

(CARETAKING) MOTHER

It was April of my 7th grade, 1965. I had a crush on a boy and on Fridays we had a combined music class. This was to be the last one and very interactive. I had really been looking forward to it. As the class began I received a message to report to the office. My aunt was waiting there. Seems my mother was afraid my father was going to kill us and she wanted me out of school.

That day it was finally made official, my mother was nuts. My aunt took me back to her house where my mother was. She didn't look good. In fact, she didn't look as though she was there at all. I could quickly tell I wasn't really registering for her. I could tell she had completely withdrawn from me and everything else. Her eyes were seriously distant. I swallowed hard as I realized how alone I now was. She had been my best friend but she was gone. I could really tell I didn't matter to her anymore. I could feel all this when I looked at her. The image is still burned in my mind's eye. I can still see her eyes. Mother, where have you gone? You're not here for me anymore, are you? In fact, it would be so much worse than even abandonment; I would become her enemy, her focus for her insane anger and hatred.

My aunt called me over and whispered that my mom wasn't doing so well. My uncle, her brother and our family doctor was going to give her some pills to make her feel a little better. The Rolling Stones would soon release *Mothers Little Helper*. This song was about this happening to many mothers. My uncle was our doctor. He diagnosed her as paranoid schizophrenic. He put her on tranquilizers. I'm sure his intention was to help but because we had very little money, he gave her all the sample packages coming in to his office. She was constantly being put on different types of the medicine. Each one gave her a different personality. And then periodically as a statement of self-assertion she would refuse to take them. Oh my god! The stuff that would start flying out of her! All the repressed rage the pills were holding back would explode all over me.

Welcome to my teenage years. After school ideally, I would have been involved in some sort of sport or activity or one of the many interests I had wanted to pursue but was told I could not. When I came home from school I was told to sit across from her at the kitchen table. She usually started with the phrase: "You're on your high horse again" and begin to criticize every last inch of my being for hours. Then she would tell me what a rotten bastard my father was and all the horrible things he had done and said to her. Daily reports and details.

Eventually as her condition continued to deteriorate the rage became overwhelming. Her eyes were completely crazy at this point, there was no focusing, and they were a strange pale blue, glazed over and totally distant. She heard voices all the time. There was the group. She believed the neighbors and her family were out to get her. She would now scream at me for hours upon hours. The words stopped making sense. The peak was once she locked me in a room at my aunt's and screamed completely incoherently at the top of her lungs in my face for five hours. No one stopped her. It was our business.

One night as I stepped out of the bath, my mother burst through the door angry as hell, aggressively grabs me by the arm and drags me into her bedroom and throws me on the bed. Billy

Graham is on the television. She screams at me: "Sit here and listen to what this man has to say and save your sorry soul. You are going to hell." Minutes later she flew down the steps and I heard a loud rattling of utensils bouncing against each other as she tore open a kitchen drawer. My survival instinct became acute, is this finally it, is she grabbing a knife and coming to kill me? I run in my room and throw on clothes and run down the steps to the front door, waiting to see if she rounds the corner with a knife. No. She doesn't come. I wait. I finally go upstairs. It's just another night with psychotic mom.

Another time I was taking a shower and believing my parents were downstairs I took a flying leap from the bathroom to my room without clothing. Unfortunately, my parents were in their room and saw me. My mother later went in my room and ripped to shreds my latest Beatle album cover, she knew where it hurts. Luckily it was *Yesterday and Today*, not too stunning. While she was in there she opened a drawer and found the four dollars I had rolled up to buy a Paul Revere and the Raiders album. I had thrown the money back in the drawer from my pocket resisting the purchase because my mother had forbidden me from spending any more money on record albums. She confronted me with the money accusing me of being paid by my father to see me naked. She screamed and yelled for hours at me, not him.

My father intervened only once. My mother went through an alcoholic phase. She was drinking a fifth of vodka a day. She made my "old enough to buy alcohol" boyfriend go and get it for her. No matter how I pleaded she would not stop screaming until I gave in. One summer day my father happened to be home when I wanted to go to my friend's house and my dad heard my mom tell me I could not go, I was to stay home and watch her get drunk. He actually stepped in and told me to go to my friend's home.

One autumn when the leaves where on the ground she began wandering around the front lawn with a shopping bag picking up the leaves she said that Jesus told her to. Lots of bags began to accumulate in her bedroom (my parents had separate rooms by that time) and the leaves began to fall out onto the floor along with various insects crawling out. The house became infested with fleas.

Often on Friday nights when I got home from a date, she would announce that we had to get out of there; my Dad was going to kill us. Years later I came to see that this was a projection; I eventually had to commit her, as she was seriously threatening my father. So we would arrive at various family members' homes late at night with me meekly asking if we could sleep there, because my father is going to kill us. Are we talking humiliation? The absolute worst was arriving at my cousins who were very wealthy which was very intimidating to me since I was so poor and ashamed of it. We hadn't seen my cousin in years. It was one o' clock in the morning when I knocked on her door with my little anorexic mother (she was proudly down to 98 pounds at five' four") hovering behind me. I'll never forget watching the mental process in my cousin's eyes as we stood there giving her the information. "Yes, you can come in." I looked in the mirror and counted 32 hives on my face and neck from embarrassment and stress.

We stayed a week. My cousin had 6 young girls so this was a very active household. My mother was completely oblivious to what I was feeling or going through and just sat in the living

KAYA JOHN

room chain smoking. I was 16 and became so self-conscious and embarrassed by my existence, I wanted to just disappear. I was feeling all the discomfort of the family members as kind as they were. Funny, I'm getting some hives writing this!

Another incident involved this same cousin's mother. When I arrived home after school my mother informed me that my father was going to kill us and told me to go to the phone booth at the bottom of the street to call my aunt because our phones were bugged. I really put up a fight this time standing in my room. I know this was one of the worst moments for me. I was at wits end trying to get her to take into account my feelings. God, I can't tell you how bad this was for me. I was totally forced to do this. She was relentless and did not care one little bit what it was doing to me. I hated her in that moment from the frustration of trying to get my needs and my feelings to register at all with this woman, my mother. Nothing, I was not a daughter. I was just an object she had to get to do what she wanted it to do. I felt so used and abused by everyone in this nuthouse for so many years. I was so weary. So weary that I had not been feeling well and had an appointment with my uncle, our family doctor that night. He told me to come over after his regular hours. I was desperate to get there.

I gave into my mother's ranting and went to the phone at the end of the street and delivered my usual line: "My father is going to kill us, can we stay with you?" "OK." My mother has me get my boyfriend to drive us and it some distance so getting back took a while so we arrive at my uncle's office a few minutes late. When I walk into his office I just burst out crying. My uncle's only response is to reprimand me for being late and tell me as cold as ice if I can't control my emotions there is nothing he can do for me. I cry harder. He becomes colder and meaner. I made what feels like the first assertive move of my life and run out of there. And no lightning struck. I wasn't punished by god for disobeying an adult.

My mother became completely dependent upon me like a child. She took my hand to help her cross the street. She couldn't be alone. I even had to accompany her to the bathroom. My father worked nights. He worked on the weekends part-time. I was alone with her day in and day out.

When we went to stay with various family members, she wouldn't give me the key to the house to be with my cats, my only saving grace and source of love. I would go to the house and tap on the windows so the cats would jump up on the sill and I could at least see them and they could see me.

I also didn't have my Beatle music which was my greatest comfort after one of my sessions with my mother or when my parents yelled at each other. My mother and father fought from the time the sun came up until way after it would set in the west. I would go to my room and take my little hi-fi speakers about a foot tall and five inches deep and lean them against my ears while I lay on the bed. I would turn the music loud enough to drown out the sound of their yelling.

Once we visited a friend and her mother who lived down the street from us. She told me part way through the night to run home and see if I could catch whoever was bugging the house and giving the cats LSD.

It was so hard for me to go against my mother. I had been a very devoted daughter. When my mother loved, there was a

divine light that shown out her eyes. I felt completely adored.
I had no way of really understanding what was happening.
Aside from my Aunt's first comments the day she first went on
the medicine, no one offered me any information, support or
comfort. No one knew how to. This was the mid-sixties, right
before the world opened up and we started to reveal to each
other what was really going on behind those suburban doors
and all the new alternative advances in therapies. I think my
family was ashamed and had no idea what to do. And I guess
that it is none of our business was a pretty strict rule.

But I was in hell. I was completely alone. I had a boyfriend, I
had friends, but no one really wanted to listen. Everyone had
their own hell going on and nobody talked about this stuff yet.
Hmmmm. Except.......John Lennon on those records. Even
that early he was starting to reveal himself. *I'm a Loser, Nowhere
Man*, and *Help*. His lyrics were real, honest self-assessments
revealing his insecurities and needs. I'm telling you, he kept
me alive. He gave me hope. And really did lead the way out.

SONGS AND HOW THEY HELPED ME

I'M A LOSER

I first heard this song when I was twelve years old, long before I knew anything about psychology. But when John sang, "I'm a loser and I AM NOT WHAT I APPEAR TO BE," my education was started. When my mind caught that line I knew he meant what he was saying and was directly communicating from inside himself to inside us. "There is one love I should never have lost" to me is a touching way of referring to his mother and first losing her when his Aunt Mimi took him from her and then ultimately when Julia died.

Lennon himself said this was his attempt to write *The Tears of a Clown* by Smokey Robinson but I feel there was a lot of what was real for him seeping out. When he writes about "being a clown and wearing a mask but underneath his tears are falling like rain" this certainly easily fits the teenage John and even the adult. I find the line about "is it for her or myself that I cry?" quite poignant if we put it in the context of Julia, her sad life with her husband Alf, losing her son and passing on so young. John talks about "pride before a fall, I'm telling you so that you won't lose all." Here is one of the early lines where he's talking to us directly about his experience and trying to help us learn through him and not have to go through the same pain. He tells us he "left it far too late," he didn't deal with his feelings and now he lives under a false persona.

When I was in high school my English teacher told us she

wanted an essay written about how a 19th century poet's work was influenced by his life. I raised my hand and asked if I could do mine on John Lennon. I used this song, *Help* and *I am the Walrus.*

HELP

OK, this is where it starts to become blatantly obvious that Lennon is revealing who he is and what he's going through. But what amazes me is the total denial the whole world goes into. Did anyone comment on the lyrics of this song? Not that I heard. Lennon himself said by keeping the song up-tempo it disguised the seriousness of the song. For me this song confirmed for me that Lennon was sharing his real self with us. And it was an important part of my own process in learning that fame, fortune and worldly success was not necessarily the key to happiness that everyone seemed to think. I truly believed that someone in John Lennon's position would not have feelings of insecurity or sadness. I felt this way but I was nobody and a nothing (or so I had come to believe), John Lennon was everything and had everything. How could we share these feelings? These feelings must come from the inside then not hinging on external circumstances. This was a revelation. A new way of seeing myself and how life really is. So what does this mean then? This began an inquiry that has ultimately lasted a lifetime but then it meant that if he shared those same negative feelings about himself but yet could create such goodness perhaps I was not a lost cause.

For John, to actually cry HELP to the entire world while he's sitting on top of it, what does this deeply tell us about what we have set up to pursue and call happiness. He had fame, fortune, and success. He had done it, arrived at the tippy top, the pinnacle - the Beatles changed the world in so many ways, yet, HELP he cried, somebody "PLEASE HELP ME."

Yoko finally did help but that took a few years to get to. An unhappy childhood can put the drive in someone to compensate for not being loved by creating the false love of world adoration but that doesn't fix the past or eradicate the original feelings. Surprise! Who knew? Lennon (I) FOUND OUT and this theme then took him deep in himself and his song writing. I believe songs like *Working Class Hero* and *Imagine* come from this same place as he progressed through life. We as humans all need to learn that happiness will only come to us when we share the world and no longer use and take advantage of each other. Security can only be found when we can trust each other and our interactions.

When John sings about when he was younger and didn't need help from anyone but those days are gone, I wonder if any of the people who knew him when he was young back in Liverpool were just amazed. We all know the stories of tough mean impenetrable John Lennon back in those days and now he's letting go of all his defenses in front of the whole world. I can imagine that there were some men and women back in Liverpool who were quite shocked that he could and would do this. And I love when he say he's "opened up the doors", this feels so brave to me, so deep, I am touched so dramatically and opened myself by his courage to say this so publicly. And what doors is he opening; again I feel this could be strong shift for him both psychologically and spiritually. Certainly he's saying he no longer can go it alone; this closed up tough guy act has run its course. He's opening his heart again to let people in who might help him with his pain. He could be starting to move towards a more spiritual energy as well. Such a universal invitation to me was part of his opening to his deeper mission of spreading the significance of peace and love.

Any Time At All

An early song of John's that I found comfort in was *Anytime At All*. He offered me the friendship and caring I was not receiving from anyone in my family or anyone in my life. "If you need somebody to love just look into my eyes"…and look into his eyes I did and found great depth and soul and solace. He was there to "make me feel right," truly. I was mostly "feeling sorry and sad" and he offered me empathy. "Don't be sad just call me tonight," which I did and he answered through his music and the joy and pleasure I found there. The vibration of his voice soothed me, quieted me, helped me to relax, I could feel it at the base of my spine and I could calm down. "Any time at all," all I had to do was put on a Beatle record and he was there for me and I felt better. I could drown out the constant fighting of my parents and all the negativity in my mind. The "sun had faded away" for me in my life at that time and John did make life shine again. His shoulder to cry on was big, it was cosmic, it was universal, many of us cried on his shoulder and he carried it for us, for the world. Even if Lennon called this song pop crap, I would say a deeper side of him came out to touch so many of us with these words, this gift of caring, this genuine soulful offer of help to so many of us. And I believe he's still there on the other side dedicated to helping humanity make our change to a kinder species as we begin to understand that we are all the same and the world will live as one…..

Nowhere Man

I have a memory of coming to a dead stop in our local five and dime WT Grant when *Nowhere Man* was blaring over the speakers in the store, loud enough for the lyrics of the song to be heard quite clearly. In the middle of all the pop gibberish being pumped out all day long suddenly is this deep message, John's revelation about himself, let alone that one could soar through the cosmos on the harmonies. "He's a real nowhere man" ....

What he could slide in over the airwaves to those that were listening! He opened up the channels with *She Loves You* and then started pouring deep spiritual psychological emotional messages down the same tube-those who really listened were changed forever, others merely tapped their feet.

For me the other significant thing that takes place in this song is he begins to interact with us personally, he asks us a question, and starts a conversation with us, "isn't he a bit like you and me?" It's like hey world, generation, human race, what are we doing with our time here, our life, don't we want to go somewhere, let's start to look at ourselves and the world we are creating, let's do this together. I am now willing to start to see myself and examine my life, let's do this together and make a better world. His deeper mission starts to reveal itself here.

Out of all the pop songs, including the Beatles, mostly up to now we hear endless angles and perspectives of love's beginning and ending but suddenly using the same communication vehicle is an invitation for deep spiritual transformation. Lennon begins his work.

For me, I hear all this, I am called by these words, and I hear everything he says, what he is asking, I look around, and I expect to see everyone in the store riveted by what they hear. But what do I see? Everyone else is looking at underwear, 45's, towels, bed sheets, what have you. Why isn't anyone else around me hearing this? Why isn't everyone else jumping up and down and excited as all get out for this opportunity we are being offered by this man, this "Beatle?"

I want to tell people in great detail how my life was changed by John Lennon, no, how my soul was, how my beliefs about myself and the world, my values and ideals. His was the most amazing and impactful life of my lifetime and his death as huge and dazzling and effectual as his life. The day the earth stood still.

I am watching the world still struggling to get to where he was many years ago. His message lives on stronger as the years pass, people recognize deep inside the truth he spoke. The power in John and Yoko's creativity is paying off more and more. The wonder of what they chose to do together, not calling it naiveté, but finally seeing the courage and genius of artistic originality.

IN THE SUMMER OF '79

In the summer of '79 I knew I had to commit my mother to the psychiatric ward of a local hospital. I had moved in with my parents and soon found out things were getting into crisis. In '74 my father became completely disabled with MS and my mother had become broken down with emphysema and of course her mental illness. So now these two who hated each other's guts were alone in the house together 24/7. At this point, my mother had to totally take care of my crippled father even though she was sick as hell, herself.

My father quickly revealed his concerns for his welfare. He told me she had already hit him in the head with a can of cleanser. (HE of course threw one at me years later). But of serious concern was she was sitting across from him on the sofa with a hammer smashing the coffee table and telling him his head was next. I saw the indentations in the table. My father was a complete cripple at this point. And of course there is a Beatle song for everything…"Maxwell's silver hammer came down across his head…"

Now my mother who has been treated so badly by him all these years must now be further humiliated by being committed. But as it was, I felt I should tell my Uncle her doctor and I think I needed him to sign some papers. He told me I didn't know what I was doing, that it was the wrong thing to do and he would have nothing to do with it……

I then informed my mother's closest sister. She basically said the same thing but told me years later what I said that day let her know I was starting to change. To her I responded: "I'm the one who knows what's going on in that house." Once again, I was showing some self-assertion.

Somehow I got someone to sign the papers. The police came and the ambulance came and they wrapped up my poor little mommy in a straightjacket and put her on the gurney and rolled her out of the house. I will never forget the vulnerability and defeatism on her face as she looked at me and whispered: "I never would have done it."

My mother had the best three weeks she'd had in years. No husband. She had some fun and creativity with Arts and Crafts. She had a professional to talk to and help her. What a concept.

It was then decided that my mother would then move in with my brother on the other side of the country, my father would move in with his son and the house would be sold, and I would be free of taking care of my parents for the first time in my life.

My mother moved and it lasted about two months, she couldn't tolerate all the commotion of my brother's family. My father called her on the phone and told her he missed her and asked her to please come home. She said yes. She arrived back home, surrendered her fate, waited on him hand and foot and then laid down one night on the couch six years later and quietly died.

Meanwhile, after being up for parole, I am sentenced to twenty more years of hard physical and emotional labor.

MOTHERS PASSING

The Christmas Angel

My mother passed from this world early one December and was escorted home by angels.

Even though my mother had been ill for many years with emphysema, there was no change to indicate the end was near before I had a vision.

At the time I was living some 250 miles distance from my parents. Though I was thirty years old, this was my first experience of living out of the state I had always called home. This was a needed step for my mother and I to begin our separating process. I would always cry after a visit home when I realized I would not see my mother again for several months.

One night in mid-November I sat down to meditate and I was immediately taken away with a vision. I walked through the door of my parent's home and approached the chair where my father always sat. I told him I knew we did not always get along but I loved him and I would always be there to take care of him. I then went and sat down next to my mother on the sofa and held her hand.

I tried to look into her face but I could not see her, I could only weep. I have since been told that this is a common sign that someone is going to pass on.

At this time I became aware of a band of herald angels encircled around the top of their house. I was startled and amazed yet thrilled they were there. But the portent was unnerving and their presence seemed to ask a question, who will be the Christmas Angel? I avoided hearing the answer though of course inside I knew.

I went about life as usual but every so often I would check in and sure enough the angels were still there. At Thanksgiving I went to spend a few days at home and noticed immediately physical changes in my mother. She had dropped considerable weight and her face had changed from that of an older woman to that of a baby. The look on her face had completely changed from one of suffering to the innocence and wide-eyed wonder of an infant. Sitting across from her at the kitchen table sharing a heartfelt discussion, I checked in and yes, the angels were right above us now.

I was going to say something about it but she was speaking and I did not want to interrupt. Also, for some reason I decided I would tell her at Christmas. Two things of note did happen during that conversation; at some point my mother turned in amazement as we were talking and told me she just saw a flash of white light. I told her that was a very high sign and not to be afraid. I then found myself sitting next to her taking her face in my hands and kissing her entire face over and over feeling my heart would burst with my love for her – my precious mommy.

That evening we watched a television program featuring entertainers over the years. I stayed late to watch the Beatles with her and left as I had to get up early the next day.

Two days later, I received a package in the mail from her. I remember I just sat flat out on the floor thunderstruck after I saw what she had sent me. The gift from my mother was a glass herald angel. My heart was thrilled but heavy. Later that night my mother's closest sister called to tell me that my mother had quietly passed away sleeping on the sofa that night. I felt that my mother had given me proof of life after death and had let me know she was safe with the angels.

In the following weeks my mother reached out to me twice. The first was on the Sunday morning after her passing. My mother was heavily into the TV evangelists. Since she was house bound, this was her church. My mother believed in and dearly loved Jesus. She was also deaf in one ear so every Sunday my mother would blast these preachers into the living room much to my father's chagrin. On this first Sunday I happened to be in the living room standing on the opposite side of the room from where the TV was located. At 9:00 sharp, the television switched on by itself very loudly as the first of her shows began. Once again I felt that she was telling me God's message of everlasting life was real and I thanked her.

My mother's next contact was on Christmas day. This was always a special day for Mom, Dad, and myself. My parents called a one day truce to their fighting and even though money was an ongoing issue, they were quite generous. To see us that day, one could believe we were a happy family. My mother always finished off the day with a traditional feast of turkey, delicious homemade stuffing, and all the trimmings.

The first Christmas morning without her, so soon after her death, was very poignant. Later in the day my father was upstairs, we were going to dinner at his son's (my half-brother). I was finished dressing and came into the kitchen for a sip of something to drink. As I entered the room I was knocked back by the aroma of turkey cooking - the smell was so strong! And when I opened the fridge it was filled with the smell of cranberry sauce and relish trays like Mom and I always put together. If I know my mother, she cooked Christmas dinner in heaven that day and some of the aroma floated down to us.

Remembering my mother when I was very young, she was an exceptionally beautiful and loving person. Her relatives confirm this for me.

Unfortunately life with my father was very hard, leading to her mental breakdown, lingering illness, and an early grave. Even through all of this she continued to take care of my father in his own illness.

I pray that all this signified an acknowledgment and honoring of my mother for the good person she is and all that she went through. I know she was truly rewarded in heaven as the Christmas Angel.

THERAPY AND TRANSFORMATION

In the fall of '74 I began my transformational work by entering Primal Scream Therapy with a local woman who I credit with helping me save my life. I had read about the therapy in a magazine and was so excited about it I ran downstairs to my mother and with great enthusiasm said: "I just read about this new therapy, that if your father didn't love you, you can get into a room and scream about it!" Behind her smokescreen of endless cigarettes and True Story magazines she looked up at me not comprehending, I went back to my room. Soon after I heard of the therapy again through John Lennon who said that it "allowed us to feel feelings continually, and those feelings usually made you cry."

Over the years I saw several therapists, lived in a spiritual community and took workshops all to help me heal and transform my life. All were helpful but the biggest memory did not emerge until the late 90's quietly on a Sunday morning.

FATHER

Why I am the way I am

"I am not what happened to me, I am what I choose to become."
Carl Jung

Early one Sunday morning sitting on the sofa, my husband sleeping upstairs, I was writing in my journal. I was in a deep place and sincerely asking God why I hurt so much and had such a difficult time in life. Truly, what is going on with me? I began to feel physically very ill, I lay down on the couch as my head began to throb, nausea overtook me and my whole body began to ache like never before. Tears streamed out of the sides of my eyes and I had a memory of being very young lying on the floor, my head knocking against it as I was being raped by my father. It took every ounce of strength to endure the body sensations I was re-experiencing. The recall went on for three hours. My husband who usually gets up at about 9:30 did not appear until after 11:00, right on time to comfort me as the feelings began to recede. I finally understood why I was the way I am, all the problems my body had. Many of my psychological and emotional struggles finally began to make sense.

My body shows what I have been through. My pelvic floor has never had any strength. It has always been impossible for me to stand for any length of time. I feel like my insides are going to fall out.

The muscles on the insides of my legs can best be described as shredded. And intolerably painful, a massage therapist worked exclusively on this area when I was living in the spiritual community. It never stopped being intensely painful. As an adolescent when I tried to use tampons I nearly went out of my mind. I nearly passed out from physical pain and the stress. When I had an IUD put in when I was married for the first time at 19, I came home and sat in a chair and stared into space for three hours.

A friend of mine gave me the book *When Rabbit Howls* by Truddi Chase, about extreme violent incest abuse, I sucked that book up. I had joined an Incest Survivors Group when I lived in a spiritual community. This was the beginning of owning these experiences for me. I felt great comfort in being there.

Some years later I was quickly transferred from one center of the spiritual community to another taking me out of my cocoon, shaking my defense system. This move returned me to living near my father a few years after my mother had passed on. I visited him the next day and when I returned to the community, I began doing some yoga. When I went into the twist posture I quietly heard my inner voice say "You were incested by your father." I had no memories at this time but I could feel and knew it was true.

I worked with a brilliant cranial sacral therapist for years who worked relentlessly to discharge the negative energy in the pelvic and leg area of my body. There were times when the release was profound as she helped me free my body from the attack still stuck inside after many years. I am forever grateful to her. She also told me that in her training she learned that the body had certain traits if incested, which I certainly had.

Years later, I gathered my nerve and I confronted my father one day while visiting him in his veteran's nursing home. It unfolded in an odd but telling way. An ongoing issue with my dad for many years had been my wanting him to turn over his house to me legally to keep it from going to Social Services to pay for his care. While living and working in the spiritual community neither my husband nor I had made any money so we really needed the home to live in and I felt I had earned it for taking care of him and mother for many years with their disabilities. He refused many times over the years no matter how much I reassured him I would not throw him out but his fear and mistrust persisted. He'd been in the veteran's nursing home for some time always believing that he would one day return to his house which he wanted for himself, not me.

So in the course of our conversation that day I asked him about the incest and he told me he never touched me. But somehow in the same conversation the length of time it took him to turn over the house to me also came up. He told me he turned the house over to me the first time I asked. I was floored but I saw the irony and connection with both issues. Turning over the house was obviously not true so I just bet what he said about never touching me wasn't true either.

I had a medium reading with psychic Deborah Rees, 10 years after he had passed on, the incest came up and my father admitted it. The depth of my terror and pain was acknowledged. I was able to receive the needed truth and healing at last.

My father's mother was married at 15, had my father at 16 and was widowed when he was two months old. She put him in foster care until he was five years old. He lived on a farm and I sense and have had this confirmed on a psychic level that he was sexually abused while he was there. I do believe these behaviors can be compulsively repeated and that is why he hurt me. I am so grateful for all the ways our society has opened up and I could get all the good therapies I have to break this pattern and heal my body and heart. And again I thank the Beatles for all the good changes their music and attitudes have brought and reflected. I believe the openness around these issues and the help now available is directly connected to the changes in the world heralded by the Beatles music.

A MESSAGE TO ME ON THE FLOOR BEING RAPED FROM MY OLDER SELF

Endure. It is worth getting through this. This is not eternity. What's happening won't last forever. This is a very sick person. This was done to him so he is doing it to you. He knows no better. He is fixated, compulsive and blind. It is nothing personal. I promise existence will be worth it overall. It'll never be this bad again. There will be lots of good. People will love you and they won't hurt you like this. I will help your body recover. We can heal the body and the spirit and the soul. We'll do it together, as long as it takes. I'll stay with you, I won't abandon you. Please hang in there. It'll be over soon. He won't do it again. Ever. He'll get help when he's dead. He'll be sorry. There will be the Beatles. Their music will cheer you; they will show you that life is worth living, that love is real, that God exists. There is purpose and goodness and reason in life. All this will come to you. People will help you along the way, and then your kind husband will come and you will finally be safe and cared for and loved. You will have joy in your life. You really will.

ABOUT MY DAD: LIGHTNING STRIKES TWICE

During the summer of 1942 my father was working for a pharmaceutical company that because of the war was making plasma out of blood that the Red Cross was collecting. The plant was working under top security, running twenty-four hours a day.

The company employed its own electricians including my dad. He was 21 and he and his first wife were expecting their first child any day. It was 5:30 on a Friday afternoon. My father was working on a burned-out motor in the maintenance building. Quitting time would be soon, his paycheck was already in his pocket.

Unfortunately a thunderstorm broke out, delaying the end of the work day. The main source than ran the plant came into a 6 foot by 8 foot switch house on the premises. The switch house had been struck by lightning and one phase of the electricity for the company was knocked out.

My dad, another worker and their foreman were called immediately to restore the power. Dad knew it would be dangerous but also knew it was his job. Having never worked with more than 440 volts, he hoped it would be just a fuse which they could easily replace.

The floor of the switch house was covered with water when

they arrived, so they covered it with wooden planks. They entered and were starting to assess the problem when a red ball of lightning, one foot in diameter, burst through the door and rolled between the men.

It hit the transformer. Four thousand volts blasted through the main switch, built to handle 440 volts. The switchboard was blown to smithereens and pieces flew out in all directions. The current hit my father's coworker in the face and charred him from the waist up, jumped to my dad and locked him into the flow of the current. The current then jumped to the foreman and killed him instantly. At that moment a lab technician ran into the switch house to see what was happening and the current jumped to him and he died on the spot.

The current then knocked my father backwards, spun him around and pinned him against seven other switches. The current was arcing from the switch to his chest, attracted to a button on his overalls. According to the authorities my dad received 2900 volts for three and a half minutes. The electric chair gives person 2000 volts for a matter of seconds.

Incredibly, my dad fought for his life. He gritted his teeth so hard that they all chipped and blood spurted from his mouth. A silver ring made from a French franc melted off his finger.

He would not let himself die. Up until then he had been a healthy, well built, good looking man. He had won athletic awards in the Boy Scouts. He thought about his wife about to give birth. He did not believe this was his time to die. He loved life and didn't want to go. He held on as long as he could but started to feel his endurance slipping away. He began to give up. He went limp.

The current stopped. My dad fell to the floor. Three men were needed to carry him out to keep his rear from dragging on the floor. While lying on the ground waiting for the ambulance, a lab technician came over to him. Father wrote his telephone number on her white lab coat. He asked her to call his wife and tell her there had been an accident. He would be all right but was going to the hospital. He was afraid that she would hear the story on the news and not know who was dead and who was alive. He never lost consciousness or mental functioning.

At the hospital it was discovered that Dad's fat tissue around his joints had been pushed out through his pores. Dad said that if anyone had asked him "What's cooking?" he would have had to say, "me!" The hospital staff took pieces of cardboard to scrape what resembled yellow chicken fat off of him before he could be bathed.

After dad was bedded, his eyes started to feel as if they were on fire. The pain was unbearable. The ultra–violet rays from the arcing had sunburned his eyeballs. He became blind. The doctors were unsure if he would regain his sight, not knowing how deeply his eyes were burnt.

Father insisted he leave the hospital the next day – he knew he would be needed at home. He went home blind and while sitting in his chair, the stiffness set in. There was no lubricant left in his joints. The burns in his chest remained weeping sores and had to be redressed every other day by a specialist.

Dad was left with a hole in his finger where the silver ring had been. You could stand a match up in it. The burns on his chest turned into two black checkers and seven scars remained on his back.

After three days, my father's eyes peeled and he regained his sight. His son was then born. Gratefully, he could see his child!

Dad went back to work in two weeks. Eventually he joined the Navy where he continued his electrical work. After his discharge, he started his own electrician business.

Finally in 1947, the event caught up with his nerves. Working on a hot wire in a tight spot, he began to shake. He felt deathly afraid. He called an electrician friend and told him he had fallen to pieces and couldn't touch hot wires again. His friend finished the job and the business was sold.

As time went on Father began to feel pain at the bottom of his spine and began to have trouble walking. He began to feel numb. In 1974 he was diagnosed with multiple sclerosis. This is a deterioration of the nerve endings that send electrical messages to the brain.

My father often showed me the newspaper article about the accident. I asked him to fill in the details for a college writing project. At the time he told me this story he walked with two canes and was 59, my age now. It is a miracle he was still alive and lived to father me.

THE CADILLAC AND THE SOUPED UP BEETLE

During my teenage years I began to use a little make up. A little Slicker lipstick from Yardley of London as advertised on the Monkees show and a little blue eye shadow on the eyelids as was the fashion.

My father barged into my bedroom one morning when we were going to the shore for the day and in his usual communication style, belligerently said. "You will not wear make up!" He then turned around and left.

I kidded myself and agreed in the moment because I would be going in the ocean. My parents were taking my friend with us so I was very excited about this day down at the shore. I loved the amusements down there and my girlfriend and I would be able to ride them together that night. It was not often that they did something like this and for me to have a companion was great. So we had our day on the beach and when we dressed for dinner I put on my eye shadow and lipstick. My father took one look at me and refused to be seen with me. I can still feel the adrenalin move through my body, the stiffness in my joints and the nausea and headache from the rejection, shame and humiliation in front of my friend. My mother took us to dinner.

We made it home. The next Saturday a guy I was dating stopped by to see if I wanted to go out that night. Sure. When I reentered the house, my Dad in his usual way said: "You're not going out tonight, you're grounded."

I told my mother what was going on and she said: "No, you're not, go out tonight,"

My father then went outside and turned his late model lime green Cadillac around in the driveway so the front end is facing out, ready to go. Hmmm.

So when my date arrived to pick me up three people came out onto the front lawn to greet him, my parents and me. My mom said "You two go out and have a good time!" My dad said: "She's going nowhere."

The guy I was going out with was not a boyfriend. This was a casual thing. He'd never spent time with my parents. He was a quiet shy guy. His face flushed and his eyes were going back and forth as his mind was trying to make sense out of what he was confronted with.

Now my parents faced each other and started screaming: "She's going out!" "Oh no, she's not!" Back and forth, back and forth, until finally my dad yells: "If she leaves this property tonight, I'll call the police." My mother retorts: "You'll call the police, hell, I'll call the police." My mother briefly left the scene and called the cops. They arrived pretty quickly but informed us this was a domestic situation which they apparently cannot be involved with. At that point my mother started screaming at the police. They threatened to arrest her if she didn't shut up. She stops yelling and they leave.

My date drove a souped up Volkswagen Beetle set up for racing. See what's coming? We hop in and take off as my father climbs into his Caddie, positioned and raring to go. We start flying down the quiet suburban neighborhood, little VW bug being chased down by a full size Cadillac complete with huge fins. At one point we came to a dead-end and my father comes around us and closes us off in front of us. My date throws the car in reverse and we zoom back down the quiet street at 40 miles per hour. The car later needed repair. We lost him.

Meanwhile, someone in one of the houses we zoomed by called the police. My dad was told he wasn't to be seen on the road again that night or he would be arrested.

Things just weren't the same between my Dad and me after that. Things hadn't been good before but this was the topper. This was probably about 1968. He never spoke to me again until he collapsed completely and needed me to take care of him in the fall of 1974.

I lived the rest of my teenage years, from age 15 until I was 19 at home and then got married and got the hell out of there with never being greeted, never acknowledged or recognized in any way. If I walked into the room, I got nothing. I didn't exist. When my best friend would come over to visit Dad would open the door one inch and then go back and sit down in his chair. My friend would then open the door, come in and sit on the couch and wait until I came downstairs to see if she arrived.

FATHERS PASSING

I was glad when I realized I did not have resentment for the young nurse my father had gifted money. I found checks adding up to $1200.00 the last year of his life. I don't know how much more he had given her over the years. What hurt was he hadn't given me a cent. My father told me that she was good to him, came and wheeled him over to picnics, that sort of thing. He wanted none of this from me so I am glad he had some companionship. She was thirty and blond, and he told me he gave her a kiss every night before he went to sleep. I know at the end she was not allowed near him. I do not know what happened but it's probably better for me that way.

At the time of my father's passing I still held onto the dream that we would reconcile and he would see the wonderful person I was and finally love me. I was even ok with a death bed scene. I couldn't believe things wouldn't end on a good note.

What happened instead was that my husband and I would visit my father once a month in the veteran's home. We would stop at several supermarkets, several fast food and regular restaurants to bring him all his favorite special foods and anything else he needed like cologne. I remember once when we were visiting him a nurse came in and asked if she could have a dab of his Brute for the man next door. Word got around he was well stocked. We had also bought him a fridge to keep the food in as well and a CD player with all his favorite big band music so he could wheel himself around listening to his tunes.

At the end of the visit I would give him the tally for the expenses and Dad would write me a check. One visit we were running late so instead I wrote him a letter with the amount $52.70 telling him when the visa bill would be due hoping that he would get the hint and send me a check which he did. Thanks, Dad.

At the end of the next visit my dad looked at me and said "Where's my $52.70? You said you needed it to pay your visa bill. Shocked, I explained that it was the money he had owed me for that month's shopping. He was furious as only Dad could be. The look of hatred and fury on his face directed at me as was as usual unnerving and defeating. I explained again and he said ok but his look told me he knew what he thought to be the truth and he knew I was a liar like he always called me and everyone else.

Thus began our new ritual of when we visited every month, he would demand his $52.70 and hit me with eyes full of distain and I would explain again and again. At Christmas I cooked him a turkey (I don't eat meat) with all the fixings mom used to make and presented it to him. I found him quite distraught and without any thank you. He only choked on his meal sending in all the nurses to save him. That effort and gesture did not go as I had intended. I found out then that he and his nurse friend were being kept away from each other; this seemed to have left him an emotional wreck. I couldn't have meant less.

At this point I finally reached my breaking point and just stayed away in January and wrote him a letter mid-February letting him know I wasn't going to visit him again. This was a life defining communication and we both knew it. I had truly had enough and was letting him and universe know it.

I was later told that when he read my letter telling him I would never visit him again he got in his wheelchair and wheeled himself out the front door of the veteran's facility and onto the road in the middle of traffic hell bent on killing himself. Someone saved him from this but he caught his death of pneumonia. So rather than reconciliation before he died, he set it up so it seemed I had sent him to his death. Deal with that, darling daughter. This haunted me for a while but I know it is not true.

Oddly enough, that weekend my husband and I were both terribly ill with serious chest colds. We just lay on the sofa at opposite ends moaning, coughing and sneezing and going round the corner to our local vegetarian restaurant for soup and food runs. On Monday we received two phone calls, one letting us know about my father's pneumonia and the other that my husband's grandfather had a stroke. According to metaphysical beliefs about emotions and the body, the lungs represent grief, so I intuitively felt we were already preparing for huge losses coming our way.

We drove down to see my dad who was lying in bed shaking like a leaf from head to toe. We stood around the bed and in a few moments he opened his eyes and saw us, I saw light and pleasure in his eyes at the sight of us and he reached up and grabbed my fingers. He said and I quote "Friends and countrymen, I will not reach 81." That's it, my father's final words, a nobleman to the end. My father is a hereditary baron of a village in England. We stayed with him awhile longer and then left his side. The next day we spent in the hospital with my husband's granddad. I was filled with anxiety that my father was dying and I wasn't there with him but no one mentioned it so I told myself this must be the way it is meant to be.

When we arrived back home about 7, we stopped at a local restaurant for dinner and both ordered a beer. When our waitress arrived she just very calmly poured the beer all over me with a look of total shock on her face. I immediately knew my father was already out and about and had seen the changes I had made to the house to make it livable against his wishes and just gave the woman's arm a little push.

When we arrived home I soon got a call from the night nurse taking care of my dad. She told me he didn't have long and I needed to handle the "do not resuscitate" recording on the phone. We did that about 9 pm. The nurse later told me that as soon as we finished she went to him and the look of pain and grimace he had on his face all day had changed to peace and softness as he took his last breaths. She called and let me know. I am really grateful such an aware and kind person attended to him and walked me through this moment. My dad and I were finally over. He was finally free of his pain filled body and his wounded soul could rest and heal.

A bit later in the evening I went upstairs into the dimly lit hallway and could see waves of energy taking form and told him "Dad, don't do it, I can't take it." Sure enough the next day the phone rang with all sorts of strange bizarre sounds when I answered it. Watching the psychic John Edward the following Monday, I had switched channels and turned off the TV when it popped back on to the Edward show to a man talking about his very difficult relationship with father and his hopes of making contact and healing.

The morning my father was cremated I awoke with a strong clear image in my mind of a truck outside our local funeral home painted purple with a huge gold crown on the side with the words "Royal Dust" across it. The initial information I was given during my first psychic reading was that my father had been the king of England in a past life. The psychic told me the king's name which was my father's name in this life. She explained he had taken it through to this lifetime as well as the royal title of Baron. Our family has been British royalty through many lifetimes.

I set up an altar for my dad on my piano. I placed a beautiful pencil portrait done of him when he was 25 as the centerpiece as well as a beautiful picture in an ornate frame with his gorgeous pompadour when he was a young boy. Pictures of he and I, his rings including his bloodstone with the naked women in gold carved along the side and his sheik head with the turban filled with jewels. Friends and family had sent lovely bouquets.

Soon after a dear friend came over to comfort me and we played my Dad's favorite song *Moonlight Serenade* by Glenn Miller. I had been playing this song every day since his death. It brought up my emotions and I cried my grief every day listening to this song. This time when I played it, my friend began to dance with me arm in arm just like my dad did when I was a young girl. My parents had always cleared the floor because they danced so well. At family weddings my dad would take me around the floor and it was happiness for me, my dad so handsome and his dancing so smooth. My friend and I both felt my dad take over one last time as we danced around the living room floor to his favorite song.

Early that summer we were having our cousin's yearly reunion at the shore and I asked if we could all go out on their husband's boat and spread my dad's ashes at sea, he being a Navy man. This we did with a wreath while passing around a bottle of my father's favorite scotch while blasting Anchors Away. I had not discussed anything about what to do after he passed with my dad; this all just seemed to unfold beautifully. I still found myself wanting to honor my father.

My husband and I had already signed on for a spiritual tour of England early that summer. Turned out we would be about an hour away from the village of my father's family ancestry and that he carried the title of hereditary Baron. My family once owned the Tudor manor home that had been torn down in the early 60's right before British Heritage started to save these glorious old mansions.

I saved some of my father's cremains and contacted the village and told them I wanted to bring the Baron's ashes to scatter in the church yard. They welcomed us at the church yard and served us tea with the villagers and family in their backyard. They gifted us with a booklet that honored the village created for the millennium. Through this I found out that our family had been given its baronhood for staying loyal to the crown during the civil war.

I also left some of my dad's ashes tied in a beautiful pouch hanging from one of the holy thorn trees in Glastonbury at the Chalice Well Gardens. I felt that I had done my very best for him.

Concerning my father's passing and John Lennon a remarkable healing took place with my cat who had suffered since birth with horrible allergies which filled up his ears with an odious brown gunk and sores all over his face. Turned out our Beatles convention was the weekend after my father's passing and my husband and I went as usual. This was the first year for an exhibit by Paul Saltzman presenting magnificent pictures of the Beatles during their stay with the Maharishi in India. As we walked into the room the first picture presented was an enormous photograph of a close-up of John Lennon looking reflective with his hand up to his face. Being totally open and vulnerable from grief from my father's recent passing I nearly went prone. A smaller but still good-sized copy of this photograph went home with us. I hung it in the Beatle/Lennon room above a cabinet. Our dear cat jumped up on the cabinet and did not leave for two weeks. He then moved onto the floor in the room for two more weeks. He was never as sick again. I am the first to admit this story sounds fantastic but it's true. He picked up on the healing energy created in that special room.

ABOUT ME

I won a beauty contest at age two. The prize was two professional 8" by 10" inch photographs, one in black and white, (the other is gonna be in colour).* I am always mesmerized when I gaze at myself in those pictures. I look like such a beautiful spiritual being. I look so soft and sweet and there is a lovely light shining from my eyes. I actually love who I am in those photos. Really love myself. It just floors me that this is me. Where is she? Where did she go? That was me?

I have a cousin who married when I four. There are movies. I am as round as I am tall. My face is totally miserable and distorted. I stayed that way. My features on my face never really straightened out into beauty again and my weight became a life long struggle. What happened to me between two and four? The violent incest had happened.

For me, walking around overweight feels like walking around naked. Everyone can see my shame. I am embarrassed about myself all the time. Everyone can see I have problems. I'm not in control of myself. Not in control of my life. I'm eating down my dysfunctions, my fears, my insecurities, my frustrations. I eat to compensate for all the disappointments and lack of creative expression. Everyone knows. Everyone can see I'm not making it in life. I can't hide my true self from anyone. . The belief about being fat is that a person is indulgent, weak and lazy, a failure of the most basic sense. Always feeling like I have to apologize to everyone I meet. I'm sorry I'm fat. I am

---

* George, Beatle Christmas Message

sorry you have to look at this. I feel sorry for my friends. They have to be seen with me. They can become fat by association. Their worth is demeaned. Can't you get anything but a fat friend? What's wrong with YOU?

I see my resistance to life. Feeling my will, that tight part of me that is constantly trying to create life the way I want it with mental power and how clenched my jaw can become. It feels like the bones in my head are hardened against each other from the mental strain.

My M.O. has been "Always wanting something other than what I have, wanting to be something other than I am, desperately trying to be somewhere else." They say the mind is creating the body, no wonder mine is tired. Feeling the part of me that holds on so tight, resists movement and change, doesn't trust that if someone changes and goes away that God will still get love through to me from someone else. It's always just God's love.

I see how my biggest life lesson is that of humility. How my negative ego hides my superiority and arrogance, how they are two sides of the same coin, the coin called ego.

And for how self-loathsome I can be, I can feel better than everyone as soon as anything goes my way or I feel the least little bit of aptitude for anything. Now they will all see me with admiration and want to be with me. Then I immediately fall out of balance and can't do a damn thing right. Ringo even mentioned this in the Anthology, that as soon as he has the thought he's doing well, it all goes to shit.

HAVING CHILDREN

From the time I was very young, I did not play with baby dolls. I played with sheep, plastic sheep. The first one I had I named Starry. I just loved her. Then there were more sheep, Goldie and Pinky and Yellowy. I sat them at tables for playing restaurant and school. I put them in beds and covered them up with blankets for nurse. I even had a nurse's outfit. I had white stockings and a navy blue cape. I loved this. I also had a set of farm animals that I played house with. I remember the chicken sitting on her nest fit perfectly into one of the living room chairs. I had a bunch of cows and of course, sheep. A psychic once told me that I had been a sheep herder in Yorkshire England in a past life. This was after I had gone there many times and decided it was the place that felt the most like home when I am over there.

My rejection of baby dolls concerns me, but it could so easily be a projection of the feelings I internalized coming at me as a baby. I remember being in 11th grade and walking down the corridor in high school with my two best friends. They started to ogle and coo and get that starry look in their eyes talking about having children. I remember thinking, what fools. Why would they want a baby? Looked like hell to me.

Over and over again I saw my friends getting pregnant and getting married. I couldn't believe they would do it to themselves. What did they think they were getting? To me it was loss of freedom which was just HUGE for me and being trapped with some guy that probably didn't treat them well and usually big financial issues. The concept of two people loving each other and wanting a baby and having the money and knowing what to do with child once it was born was beyond my ken. Never saw it. I only knew what not to do. I was terrified of having sex for fear of pregnancy. I just knew I could never handle the pain of childbirth or the emotional responsibility of raising a child. I always felt the child would quickly overpower me and we would both be in trouble. And the idea of being abandoned by the father and left on my own financially to raise kids really scared me. Once again I must have internalized my own situation though I have no conscious memories of the thought process or decisions made.

I also remember reading when I was delving deeply into feminism that women keep having more babies so that the child is dependent on the mother which translates in their minds as love. And also as the man withdraws his affections, women keep having more babies out of loneliness. This seemed very real truth to me and I wasn't falling for it. I loved cats. All my life I loved cats. All I ever wanted was cats. You want something cute and cuddly to love you? Get a cat. And when you want to go out, you're out the door.

My husband I met in a spiritual community in January. We were married in July and because we married so soon we were considered a high risk marriage. I became pregnant in October. The community greatly discouraged children and so soon in a high risk marriage was really frowned upon. I was terrified. We were in our mid-thirties and had no money of our own. I felt I had really found someone who would be kind to me but the marriage and even the relationship was still new. I was concerned about the effect of the stress of a baby would have on us. . I remember I let myself get into it for one night, feel the "la la" feelings of having and loving a baby but when I woke up in the morning it was very clear what I had to do.

So without telling anyone we went to an abortion clinic. What we found out was I had fibroids so big that I needed to be hospitalized for the abortion. We then needed to tell the authorities at the community to get the needed funds. So the night before the event my husband and I did a special meditation. I asked the baby to return to heaven and had a clear sense of the child turning into a butterfly and flying back to heaven. I feel a little emotional still writing this. When the procedure was done the next day, the doctor told me the life in the fetus was already gone. The fibroids had grown into my uterus; I would never be able to carry a child to completion.

I then had my tubes tied and a few years later developed cervical cancer. Some people believe that cancer can develop in parts of the body that have experienced trauma. I was 39. We were living with my father at the time which was necessary for me to stimulate the memories of the past but I think the stress was too much for my body. I always thanked my husband for having the courage to come with me to the lion's den so I could recall enough to heal.

Part of me was actually relieved when I had the cervical cancer and had to have a hysterectomy, now it's official, I can't have children. No one can fault me or call me an unnatural woman. Bring on the cats! Mostly I feel the desire to hold and cuddle when I see animal babies. The same feelings I see most woman express for human infants I feel when I see kittens, puppies and just about every kind of furry animal's offspring.

The whole idea of pregnancy and child rearing couldn't possibly be seen in a positive light given the circumstances of my birth and the violent incestuous abuse I experienced. The most I could do was protect myself and not hurt a child by repeating history. I observe my yearning sometimes when my husband and I see hippie kids in their twenties and joke about adopting them. We've got a whole bunch of them! I often say give me another ten years and I'll be ready!! When I experience the pleasure I feel from loving and providing for my cat and dog, I can get a glimpse of how joyful it must be to create a good life for another person if one is healthy enough oneself to do it.

There was an excellent book I read in high school by Sammy Davis Jr called *YES I CAN*. The title still reverberates in my mind working to offset so much in my life when I was told as I child about who I am and what I can do and have.

I remember myself as being very creative as a child. I drew all the time. My cats were often my models. I loved fashion design. And I often would find the fashions I drew in the newspaper not long after. In those days they had those ads in magazines, draw this picture and be eligible for a scholarship to art school. I drew a dog until it was perfect. My mom sent the wrong ones in, I was turned down. She said she was sorry but never turned in the correct ones. I asked my mother for art lessons but she told me they weren't for me. We were the working bees. That's what her mother told her.

I used to dance myself silly. There's nothing I love to do more than dance. I asked for dancing lessons. My mother told me we were the working bees.... Oddly, my best friend was one of the most privileged girls in town. I'm not kidding. She lived two doors down from me and we played together all the time.

She could play six musical instruments by the time she was six. She took art lessons and dance lessons. The absolute worse for me was being taken to her recital where girl after girl my own age came out on stage and danced their hearts out while I sat in the audience with the adults. I can still see one girl in a red sequined jacket and bowler hat tap dancing around a suitcase. I so desperately wanted to be her. I really think some part of me disassociated that day. Where could I stuff these feelings? The show lasted for a long time as girl after girl came out on that stage and danced. I just went nuts shoving down the pain.

I loved to sing. My favorite was *The Sound of Music*. And I would even sing them outside. My father had a little mound of dirt outside and I would stand on top of it and belt out *Climb Every Mountain*. I asked my mom for singing lessons; she said something about worker bees.... I remember once in singing class in grade school the teacher said she was going to come around and listen to each of our voices. I was sure I would be discovered. This did not happen. A psychic told me years later that in a past life I was a world class singer who toured Europe.

I was always trying to create backyard carnivals and plays. I would try to get my neighborhood friends involved but not too much became of it. Once I did organize a little something but I had to give everyone money to use at the various stalls and food vendors of cotton candy and snow balls!

I always loved music and wanted to play the piano. My brother being ten years older than me, was very musical, playing the trombone, French horn and accordion. We had a piano for him that I yearned to play. My mother taught me how to play the old song by the Ink Spots: Java Jive (*I Like Coffee, I Like Tea*). She sang the lyrics slightly different: instead of "I like the java jive and it likes me" she sang "I like the boys and they like me!" I waited for my brother to go to college so the piano would be mine. One morning as I came down the stairs the piano was going out the door. I shrieked: "Where is the piano going?" My mother replied: "Your brother is going away, what use we would have of it?"

As an older adult I began to take lessons. I soon realized I only wanted to play Beatles music. It is another avenue to experience their songs. I really felt the emotion of the song. I actually wept the first time I played *And I Love Her, Here There & Everywhere and Imagine.*

I sometimes have suspicions about my mother. I understand that we did not have much money and that is why I was not able to take the lessons that I wanted. Perhaps it was shame that kept her from just telling me that. But what she did do with telling me those things were for other people, to hear that we were the worker bees that left me feeling an extreme lack of confidence in my worth. I was left with a relentless voice inside saying "I Can't" when faced with any opportunity or desire in life.

I don't know if there was a part of her that did not want me to succeed because she felt so bad about herself and was so unhappy. I did internalize this. I really think I became stupid in a lot of ways for my mother so she didn't have to feel bad about her life. I joined her in her sadness and failure as part of being her friend. Not only did I not want to threaten her by succeeding, I actually joined her in her misery. How's that for loving someone? Not wanting to see the pain my success or happiness caused? Or maybe even the withdrawal of love or rejection? My mother often told me how she was ridiculed in class when she read out loud because she mispronounced words. At the time, I was an excellent verbal reader but I started doing that. I could hardly believe it myself. My mother always bumbled things because of her self-consciousness and lack of self-confidence. I did not start out that way, far from it, I remember. I had lots of ideas and lots of energy. But I got clobbered until I lay down on the couch and didn't move.

I often wonder if there was not a touch of Munchausen's Syndrome by Proxy. When I first heard of it I shuddered inside. My mother fed me ungodly amounts of food and sugar. I even found a letter from her mother expressing concern because she fed me large adult portions of food. Worse was the sugar. No limit. There were cartons of soda per week and snack cakes out the wazoo. My mother's claim to fame in life was her delicious pies and cakes. She told me she put extra sugar in everything. She felt embarrassed to tell me this but I didn't even understand that was bad, why not, it tastes better! But I was sick all the time as a kid. I recognize the feelings in my body now when I OD on sugar. It's the same. I was really sugared out from a young age. I was either comatose from the dose, withdrawing and sick or needing the next big hit. I have a memory of finding mother's amazing chocolate fudge from Christmas months later with mold on the top and she scraped it off so I could go to town. I remember just putting mouthfuls of pure white sugar in my mouth and letting it melt down my throat. I remember bowls of ice cream with pineapple topping and then a packet of saltines. And then back to sweet. Then I would fall into precious sleep.

Sometimes I think she kept me sick because she wanted me home with her. I missed about 80 days of school a year which I spent mostly laying on the couch in a sugar daze coughing and spitting up mucous. She was totally lonely. No friends, only her family who also eventually rejected her for bizarre behavior. She couldn't drive. No friendly neighbors. Her suffering was overwhelming. My heart ached for her.

I can see that it's all about creativity. I really got stunted when I was a kid and I had many natural creative abilities that got all jammed up inside.

Look at who I admire, like Lennon, very creatively expressing people. I see now why we worship rock stars and movie stars and dancers and athletes. They get to express themselves and be creative, lucky them!

But then, this is where the connection with the Beatles begins. Through all the serious physical and emotional pain and countless disappointments I never physically hurt myself or took my own life. I drank and smoked too much pot for a few years which hardly sets me apart but took nothing stronger over time. I never needed rehab. I never got a DUI. I am not on anti-depressants. I have a kind, supportive and love filled marriage. I can claim I am basically a cheerful upbeat person. I believe my home reflects the love and beauty I feel inside of me. I can clearly say I owe this to the Beatles and the teachings, inherent joy, inspiration and encouragement I found in their music both as the Beatles and individual artists, I truly dare not think where I would be today without them or where I'd be in this crazy little world either.

WHEN LIFE SENDS YOU LEMONS, MAKE LENNONAID

Because I cry......

You can trust me at my word
Tears give my character authenticity &
my emotions integrity
I don't need to play head games with you to hide
my true feelings
Tears cleanse our bodies, hearts and minds
Tears transform us-take us to a higher
level of existence
They move us along the cosmic ladder
Tears free us from where we are stuck emotionally from hurt
so that we can face life again and try again from a higher place
to live our life and love
Tears come from the core of my inner strength-they keep me
real and
in my compassion and connection to others
Tears bring relief and freedom and connect me to my heart
I love me for my tears
I fell in love with my husband because I saw him cry
I knew he could be trusted

LYMPHEDEMA

On July 6 (the anniversary of Paul & John's meeting) 1992 I was operated on for cervical cancer. Often the body breaks down in disease at the sight of trauma. I believe this went back to my abuse as a young child. My uterus was completely eaten into by tumors and hanging off of it growths the size of a grapefruit and pear. My lesion was only a half of centimeter but the doctor did a lymph dissection that compromised my lymph system leaving me with a serious medical condition called Lymphedema. I was 39.

When I was wheeled into the operating room I weighed 123 lbs. After the operation I weighed 141 lbs. My belly was protruding leaving me confused considering all that had just been removed from there. I also practiced yoga and could spread my legs and touch my forehead to the floor. After the operation, I would lean down about an inch and go into pain. I noticed that my right leg and foot especially my big toe now felt weaker and tight. In October of 99 my right leg swelled and I was eventually diagnosed with lymphedema. In the next few years it spread all around my body. I have golf ball like swelling under my arms and behind my knees. I have watched my body turn into a water bed. Fatigue is the number one symptom along with headaches, weakness and pain from the swelling. I have to wear a thick nylon garment from my foot to the top of my leg every day. Evenings consist of various large devices worn on the leg to help ease the swelling.

This has had great impact on my life. My work was very

physical and managing that and everything else one does in a day became a serious challenge. Just getting through the day was all I could do, walking any distance became painful and exercise was beyond me except for yoga. I began to gain weight from the swelling and lack of movement and also my food choices which revealed depression from my situation. I had worked very hard to change my diet and exercise to keep my weight normal after my childhood issues. Do you remember the childhood game of *Chutes and Ladders*? Right before the finish line there is a spot if you land on it, it chutes you all the way back to the beginning. This is what that felt like to me. I have enough vanity to feel embarrassed about the weight gain and the ugly thing on my leg.

Why am I telling you this? I want to raise awareness of what can happen to women/people by doctors. I really did not understand enough of what was going to happen to me in this operation to take care of myself. I am told that now they only take one lymph node, as that is all they need, rather than what my PT said at the hospital: "He killed you." Oddly enough after I had scheduled my operation with my original doctor, I had been put in touch with a doctor from England named John who told me he would do the operation vaginally. My original doctor called me and kept me on the phone for 45 minutes explaining to me that I should not do this, that I had cancer and needed a lymph dissection. My cancer was a half a centimeter, what were the chances? This has been a serious or detriment in my life. I believe another effect of the abuse I experienced as a child.

I ultimately believe that everything is working for our highest good even if I often wish I was working at a higher level so my lessons did not have to be so harsh. When I ask myself how this served me, I must admit that it really helped me clean up my act. I could no longer tolerate alcohol as my body cannot clean itself properly anymore. As much as my diet slipped from depression I am committed to eating cleaner which has lead me to a vegan diet. This will give my body as much energy as it possibly can. I was also helped by many body therapists including a Physical Therapist who specifically learned about lymphatic drainage massage to help me. I had an opportunity to again experience support and kindness.

I do feel that life has lessons to be learned. I pray for the day when we cross over into the energy of love so our lessons need not be so painful to grow. That we just keep compounding our creativity, artistic expression and good will towards all life.

MEDIUM READING WITH DAD AND MOM OCTOBER 2011

In October of 2011, more than nine years after my father's passing, I had a reading with English psychic medium Deborah Rees. It was the healing that I had prayed for and worked towards my whole life. This transcript confirms both the events and my feelings of the experiences of my childhood and my parent's present understanding and change of heart. This brings my personal history in this writing to a finish. After I received this reading I knew I could finish this book because my relationship with my parents had been rectified and healed. I intended this writing to not be a victim story but one of empowerment and growth for all who read it.

One of the main reasons I have shared my story is to let people know that even though a person has crossed over, the relationship can still be healed and transformed. This is significant and helpful for people to understand. We are still available to each other even when someone has passed on. There is still emotional and spiritual growth on both sides of life. We can always extend forgiveness to each other. Healing has no bounds!

I share this with much gratitude and thanks to Deborah Rees. She begins:

Deborah: "One of the first things I get is even though you are very softly spoken, composed and together; you've had SUCH a

65

life. Can you understand that? Which totally belies the way you appear. You appear like you would have had a nice upbringing – that everything was calm, that everything was wonderful and I don't get that from you. Can you understand that Dad is passed over? I'm going to bring him in first. I don't know who else is there but I am going to start with Dad. As soon as I said the name Dad, I got loads of emotion from him. He gives me the feeling there is loads of history between you. It's not just father and daughter. He gives me the feeling of regret (from Dad). I feel as if you were a very shy little girl is what he tells me – you were shy and introverted and I also feel that sometimes you would have been nervous of dad. I want you to know that as he comes in here, he feels very humbled to me. I feel in life he would have been like a bull, can you understand that he gives me the words raging bull. It's important (and he makes me cry) that he comes in humbly for you – so that you know where he is right now – I got a lovely feel to him – I feel he says to you: "your heart is so pure and so sweet." The feeling that he gives me is that despite everything you didn't turn hard, you didn't turn callous – can you understand this cause you could have easily turned to stone.

I feel like your Dad would have hit your Mom and there was alcohol. He was very insecure; he was so vulnerable so he had to come across as tough. He gives me the feeling that he reached in, took your sense of self-worth and threw it away, does that make sense? And you've been dealing with it ever since.

He's so proud of you, not something he ever would have said to you.

He wants you to know that the vulnerable side of him that

we were just talking about; that when he looked at you, you mirrored back to him his vulnerability-you were so soft and sweet and shy, all the things he couldn't deal with in himself. He looked at you and saw that and this is why he was so..... he didn't want to be reminded of his own vulnerability. To be honest I feel this is all about his own upbringing, not that this is giving him an excuse, again he says you didn't turn like him, why did he have to turn like that then?

He's very dressed up to come see you today. Do you have your own business right now? I get a proud feeling.

Can I tell you you're very much like your mother in temperament? Mom is- she's not like your dad, she's softer."

ME: "Yes, her essence."

Deborah: "The two of them are here together - which you might find surprising - it's different in the spirit world. They appear like doctors who want to come in and mend you - because of them- that there wasn't any softness or love - they didn't put their arms around you and tell you that they loved you - do you understand that? There were moments of that but there was so much other. They say that if they gave you a hug there was so much resentment there from you because of all the other stuff. Although I get that mom is more positive then dad but a double edged sword, she's soft then she's not. That's crazy making for a child, sometimes it's easier to deal with a raging bull, at least you know what you are getting. Out of everything they just want you to know and they get it and they get it on all the levels - they need you to know that.

Your mother's mother is there. You didn't have an adult life with her, memories are going back. You didn't really get any softness from anywhere."

ME: "Not from her."

Deborah: "I'm not sure this lady is soft either. She was strong too and felt children should be seen and not heard, don't run around, don't play with that. The whole message, they loved you but their own stuff was getting in the way of that, they are all like: Ahhh, what were we like?! It just doesn't seem fair to me but they give me the feeling that what it has done is make you strong and make you strong enough to write your story. We actually ask for the childhood before we get here. It was for a reason but they don't want that to take anything away from themselves, they don't want to say this is the way it is, they could have been better.

Was there any abuse with you? Is this with Dad? And it was sexual abuse? I feel here we have to acknowledge that and it feels - this is why he wants to take responsibility for everything - it has all gone quiet and he wants to give you the intensity of his regret about this. I feel it happened to him. He wants to acknowledge that, has he ever acknowledged it before?"

Me: "No."

Deborah: He just gives me the feeling that he's acknowledging it and whatever he can do on every level of your being to make up for that - he's going to try and do that. He gives me this: you were scared, does that make sense?

ME: "Yes, it was violent."

Deborah: "You were scared but not just the violence but underneath too, the feeling core scared, terrified to the core, not cause of the violence but cause of the actions, it's a terror is what it is. Since he has passed obviously he can feel your feelings and hear your thoughts and he's gone right back to these times and felt it from your angle. So when he says he knows, he knows, he gets it, he's felt it and he's making me cry. Sometimes the hardest thing for us when that happens is the other person understanding what they've done and on what level so it is important that he says that.

The future's bright. It feels heavy right now, a little bit depressed–can't see light at the end–it's for a reason–feels like you're in a void at the moment where nothing is happening–they give me the feeling of the song *The Rose*."

PSYCHIC EXPERIENCES WITH THE BEATLES AND JOHN LENNON

My psychic experiences started when I was 13 and in the 8th grade. I was invited to a party and I was excited because my cousin's boyfriend was going to drop me off and he had a red mustang. I had a dream that I got into the car and there was a new Beatle record on the radio. The song was sung by John. It was neither fast nor slow, a medium tempo and it was about land or sea or something like that. I went into school the next day to tell my Beatle fan friend this dream and a few months later the Beatles released *Paperback Writer* and *Rain*. It was pretty startling and exciting. That continued for many years. I had dreamed most of *Sergeant Pepper* before it came out. The first song to come through was *Within You, Without You*. The song used mostly Indian instruments which were new to me so the song sounded very confusing to me. Once I heard it on the album, I recognized it, understood it and loved it musically and for its profound lyrics.

The next experience was years later when a friend of mine and I went to the Fest for Beatle Fans in 1977 at the Statler Hilton, across from Madison Square Garden. We had a special experience. It was about one o' clock in the morning on Sunday night after the Fest was over and there weren't too many people left. We were wandering around the hotel and entered a room that was empty except for a baby grand piano and a few chairs. Within a few moments a "Lennonish" looking kind of guy came in and said, "Oh, a piano. Would you like me to play?"

We said, "Sure." He said: "I only know two songs. They're both by John Lennon." We said: "Play." He sat down and gave us a Carnegie Hall quality performance of *Imagine* and *Love*. They were instrumental and I felt the music all through my body, touching the strings of my heart. I remember tears falling out the sides of my eyes and truly being lifted to ecstasy. When he was finished he just looked at us, we were rendered speechless, and left the room never to be seen again.

We went back downstairs and were standing at the doors of the hotel looking out into the night. It was late but it was New York so the streets were still busy. There were three cabs lined up in our view that were waiting for passengers. As we were standing there I became aware that the window of the center cab was changing. A line went around the windows edge and the window became more like a TV screen. Inside was now John Lennon.

And he was being playful John, making funny faces, waving his hands and head around. So I was thoroughly enjoying myself for a few minutes but then suddenly my mind came in and asked what in the name of god is going on? So at this point I said to my friend. "Gee, there is really something funny going on in one of those cabs." She said: "Yes, I know the one in the middle. John Lennon is in it." At that point I noticed someone was approaching the cab at which my friend commented, "He's going to be leaving soon, a woman is getting in the cab." With that, the line around the window disappeared, the cab driver was back, the passenger entered and the cab drove off.

A few of the lines from John's song *Mind Games* come to mind: "Yeah, we're playing those mind games, projecting our images in space and in time. Keep on playing those mind games forever, raising the spirit of peace and love." Yes, thank you.

The next incident I recall was after John died. A friend and I were in New York. We went to the Dakota, the apartment he lived in with his family. As we walked along the side of the building suddenly there were all these pieces of paper blowing in the wind and some of them landed on the ground not too far from me. I could not see what was on these papers but I instantly knew exactly what they were. They were the signed and returned petitions included in the *Sometime In New York City* record. It was a petition to keep John Lennon in America when they were trying to deport him (that didn't work so they shot him instead). I just started to grab them and so did my friend. This led us to follow the trail of where these things were coming from so we turned the corner to the back of the building and was confronted with a true mountain of green trash bags. Stuck somewhere in the middle of all these green plastic bags was this small cardboard box with a stack of these petitions. When we started to look through the papers that each of us ended up with, I found that the addresses I had were from my local area and also from the locale that I went to college. My friend was from an entirely different part of the country and hers reflected that geography. It amazes me that even the right ones for each of us fell into our hands. I still have them, of course.

There is one other Dakota trash story. When I realized I was moving into the spiritual community I had been involved with someone for many years though it was mostly now a friendship but I wanted to be sensitive about telling him about the move. John's birthday was coming, I had the sense that I should tell him then. When we got together I had this pretty important news for him and he had this little gift for me. Someone that he knew was wandering around the Dakota and had come across another little exciting trash stash and actually found some clothing which could have been John's. This guy really did need clothing at the time so he put it on. He started to tell my friend about this so my friend started to tell him about me and how much I admired John Lennon. The fellow looked at him and said "Well, this must be for her." It was a copy of Rolling Stone magazine addressed to John Lennon. It felt like Lennon was affirming my moving into the ashram. I was getting closer.

CONNECTING

Connecting with the Lennon family really began with the spiritual community I lived in for seven years. A friend of mine had been taking some yoga classes led by teachers from the community and shared with me the program guide. I noticed a weekend course in macrobiotics, a healthy diet I had been very interested in learning about so we went the first weekend of December 1982. There I was to hear the community's spiritual teacher give several discourses and really found someone who had something to say to me. I got the tapes of the weekend and listened to them many times. I found great wisdom. I then noticed in the program guide there was a month long program that June (1983) that sounded just right for me. I made plans to go on retreat. I will always remember that warm summer evening as I sat outside on the picnic table, under the trees by the lake and ate my first delicious meal of black bean and carrot soup. I had found a haven. For one month I was free of taking care of my sick and crazy parents, I did not have to waitress and there would be no alcohol or drugs (my rehab, perhaps). Sanctuary.

I will always remember that month with gratitude. It changed my life. I remember in the morning before class I would take this wonderful walk up a shaded dirt road to a farm where a sweet light gray cat with striped legs and blue eyes would greet me while I watched the sun shine on a flock of pigeons flying in perfect formation. The retreat center had gardens full of purple petunias that I would always stop and bend down and smell their heavenly fragrance and feel their velvety texture.

To this day I surround myself with them in summer. I received massages by the lake where I could hear the ducks faintly quacking and splashing as they landed in the water. I was ready to give up chaos in my life. I wanted peace.

After the month, I would come up on weekends whenever I could. I would take yoga classes, maybe hear a lecture by the Yogi, walk and sleep on a balcony under the stars. This I really loved, I was far enough out in the country to really see the night time sky. I reveled in waking up throughout the night to the scene above me.

The sad news or so I thought was that as of November 1, they were closing this branch and moving to another state 250 miles away. I went up the third weekend of September believing it the last time, as it was getting too cold to sleep outside. I remember I brought enough money to treat myself to one last book and cassette tape. What happened instead was I woke up in the morning knowing I was moving with them. The turn of the wheel had quietly happened while I was sleeping. I did not think about it, there was no decision process involved. I just knew this was what I was to do. So somehow in the next five weeks I was to get my parents and cat taken care of, and leave my job. I could barely take a deep breath but it all got done.

Upon beginning that day I realized I needed to talk to someone about doing this. Turned out there was just one bed left. Amazing. This is where the Lennon karma began. When I asked if there was someone who could talk to me about going there, I was told that JULIA would talk to me. Being the Lennon fan that I am I was struck right away, Julia being John's beloved mother's name and I had never met anyone with that name. Turned out when I sat down with Julia the first thing

I asked her was where we were going. She told me Lenox (Lennon?). So Julia was telling me how to get to Lenox. The significance did not escape me.

The big day of November 1 1983 soon arrived which began my seven year stay at the yoga retreat center. It was like being on another planet. I was learning a new perspective on life and a new set of behaviors. I was in a different state; I left my parents, my boyfriend of 9 years, my job, my cat and all my friends. I worked six and half days a week, starting with yoga and meditation at 5 AM. There was an evening lecture at 7, lights out suggested by nine. And I was de-toxing like hell. I was sick for years.

On the drive there to move in, the odometer in my car turned straight nines, John Lennon's lucky number. Soon after my arrival I was down in the basement and on a shelf was a magazine that was open to an article on the Beatles. I was thrilled. John was letting me know he was here. I wasn't completely alone. Also, my lucky number is 7 and after exploring the area I discovered that there was both a Rt7 and a Rt9 and they intersected. Lenox, where 7 meets 9, I was becoming intrigued. Next they started to build a new restaurant in town; I soon discovered its name was The Dakota, the name of the apartment building the Lennon's lived in. Its telephone number was filled with sevens and nines. In December I was to meet my closest Beatle friend. We both had told the same person that "John Lennon was my first guru" so he introduced us.

I was also told by someone that John had rented a house nearby that my friend and I went to see. I bought a book a few months later while visiting Liverpool (my first trip to England was actually May of 84, I left the ashram for a month) with pictures of them at the house sledding!

In November of '84 I went home and had a psychic reading. We talked of my John Lennon connection. She told me the day before she had done a reading with a woman who was one of the closest friends of the man who took over as Sean's nanny after John's crossing. She said "on this same vibration you have come today."

By John's birthday October 9th in 1985 I had a good bunch of friends and a very wonderful roommate. We had all planned to go out that night and listen to the words of wisdom of John Lennon's last interview and stop at our favorite drugstore soda fountain for hot fudge sundaes. Turned out my roommate wasn't feeling well so four of us went and when we arrived at the drugstore we were informed that the fudge machine was broken. We then drove to the nearest Friendly's but the line was too long to endure. I still remember one of the women yelling to me: "Will you please have your guru tell you where he wants us to go?" So I tuned in inside and got the answer, "The Dakota!" So we drove to the restaurant, none of us ever having been there, and I asked if they by chance had hot fudge. "We sure do, we serve mud pies for dessert topped with hot fudge." They let us sit in the lounge and we totally indulged ourselves. This was a major treat for us given our very healthy diet at the ashram.

Upon my return after a night of listening to John's music and philosophy and a yummy tummy I returned to my room. My roommate told me she wanted to tell me something. She let me know that one of her closest friends from high school had been working for the Lennon family as a gardener and caretaker in

Florida for a few years before John's passing. Since that time he had moved into the role of Sean's nanny. He had been asking her to get together. Would I like to meet him? I could join them. I quietly said yes. I will never forget the feeling as my head landed on my pillow. It was the softest landing of my life. Some part of me calmed down so deep inside, I felt so satisfied and so grateful. Finally, contact. (Some years later I was working with a spiritual counselor who was confirming my connection with John but said it had caused me much pain that he never contacted me in the physical in this lifetime. I experienced the strongest outburst of tears in my life).

And oddly enough, my friend who connected me with the community through the yoga class had tried to help me meet this same person a few years before. Turns out he had met someone who was good friends with the caretaker on their Florida estate. Eventually a plan was put into effect that when John went down there the following January, we would be called and down to his estate in Florida we would go. Instead December 8th, 1980 happened.

But now I was to meet this person, anyway. The plan would be that my roommate and I would travel together back home for Thanksgiving and meet her friend in New York on the way home. That was December 2nd, 1985. Turned out on TV that same night was the premier of the John and Yoko story talked about for years, so after lunch we zoomed back up north to the home of a friend where a whole bunch of us watched that story together. Also, the night before I stayed up late watching an entertainment special on TV sitting on the sofa with my mother. The last segment we watched was the Beatles. I called her a few days later to tell her all about meeting Sean's nanny.

On the 6th of December, she passed on. This is the timing of things.

As my roommate and I pulled up to the Dakota Apartment in NYC, Sean's nanny walked out the door and hopped in. He glared at me. Oh no, I thought, he doesn't want to know me! We drove a short distance to the Tavern on the Green and I went into the restroom. In there I looked at myself in the mirror and realized I could not bear how much I wanted him to like me. I willed myself to switch my mind which I miraculously did and by the time I sat down I didn't care who the hell he was and what he thought of me. All went well. We went to Strawberry Fields after lunch and my roommate took some wonderful photos, her being a professional photographer.

That began a gradual progression of getting closer to the Dakota and the family. For several years I would stop by either coming or going from visiting my father. The first time Sean's nanny brought out John's dog, a Japanese Aikido, a big friendly soul who as we sat on a bench, at the Imagine Mosaic in Strawberry Fields straddled me and gave my face a full licking. Well, it wasn't John but one is grateful for what one gets. Next visit, he took me into the office. As we were walking down the hall he whispered in my ear "Well, you've made it to the office." The walls had some beautiful pictures. Seeing the file cabinets filled with all that John & Yoko & Sean had produced was exciting for me. Then the day came when he asked me to drive him to pick up Sean at a birthday party at Chuckie Cheese. He was about eleven and adorable beyond words. When we pulled up at the Dakota there were a bunch of young girl Sean fans oohing and ahhing over him. I saw a touch of the adoration from the other side. He handled it well.

Another visit where I saw Sean's nanny was when I was to go to the office of the Dakota and call for him. I will never forget what it was like to walk up those same steps that John struggled up with bullets in his back. I put my arms on the marble counter where he had collapsed. To just walk down the passageway where he was shot felt so heavy. The thrill actually standing outside John Lennon's apartment door ringing the bell. I had made it. I had set my sites at 11 years old and here I was, 22 years later. I entered and thought, "OK Lennon, let's have you" (line from a Hard Day's night) but alas he had been gone for five years. Oh my. But I did get to twang his guitar and pluck the keys of the white grand. I lay on his couch and watched the movie *Legend* (fitting title) with his three cats laying on me. (He had bought 4 but one fell out the window, how foreboding) Later that night I put the ear phones on and listened to the Beatles on CD in Sean's nanny's apartment, a floor above the Lennon's. In the morning I sat in John's favorite chair and ate breakfast. Sean's nanny showed me John's favorite breakfast bowl but could not let me use it! I then got to go over to Julian's apartment and found there a six-foot long file of every picture of John Lennon ever taken. Pictures I had never seen and ones that captured him really close up.

Next I remember I was meeting the nanny and he told me to stand outside because Yoko was coming down. What I remember is her passing by and getting into her limo, then looking up at me and saying, "Are you Kaya?" I said: "yes," and she got back out of the car and shook my hand. I said some profound thing about it being an honor to meet her or something. I remember how slight she is, about 4' 11", 98 lbs, but yet the feeling of solidity and power was overwhelming. I was thrilled.

Eventually his nanny brought Sean to our community in June of '88. This was amazing. I actually gave him a facial! Looking down on that boy's face, he has his father's eyebrows completely. After the experience Sean filled out an evaluation that I still have. To the question "what made you decide on this service?" He answered: "Kaya's good looks and charm" and to the question Could anything have been done better, he answered: "No, seldom does one experience such perfection in a lifetime." What a hoot! We also went to the movies. And I actually got to do some caretaking, attending to a hurt foot. Over the years, Sean's nanny was very good to me sending me lots of goodies: Lennon stuff being put out by the estate, autographs and pictures of Sean and a copy of John's book: *Skywriting by Word of Mouth*, autographed to me from Yoko.

My biggest gift was when he stayed at the community for a few weeks in the summer of '87 and gave me the gift of a beautiful silk blouse of Yoko's that looked like a monarch butterfly. He gave it to me on the morning of the Harmonic Convergence, a significant spiritual day. Butterflies always symbolized deeply the transformation in myself that I am working on in this lifetime and it was really a comfort to me when I was diagnosed with cancer. Sean's nanny was even at the spiritual community the day I married my husband and I have a wedding gift both from Yoko (An autographed plaque of her most beautiful writing) and Sean (a drawn picture wishing us lifetimes of happiness). I am truly blessed and awed.

ABOUT JOHN

HOW IT WAS FOR ME

Before the Beatles I couldn't even relate to the way people looked. I thought boys were the ugliest things I had ever seen. They all had short little brush haircuts with pimples on their foreheads from the wax they put on the front hairs to make them stand up. Women were wearing beehive hair sprayed hairdos and silly glasses. No one felt touchable to me.

The world I knew had very little color. Men wore white shirts and black pants. The color purple didn't exist. I remember seeing a Jerry Lewis movie and he was wearing a pink shirt. It struck me as incredible that a man would wear a pink shirt. Our house was devoid of colors. We were poor by American middle class standards. Our furniture was hand me downs from my uncle the doctor. The house was mostly gray and brown. I slept in a bedroom with brown patterned wallpaper. The living room had gray wallpaper and gray rugs, the cheap little shags from back then that couldn't stand up at all on their own after you walked on them. Things were pretty drab.

John Lennon had so much energy emanating from him. He seemed to be blowing out all the chakras at full hilt. I remember reading early on that he hated "thick people." I really related to that and remember a story of a reporter being condescending to him and somehow leaving the reporter with something in his mouth and both hands full and he walked away. He did not "suffer fools gladly" whereas I really was suffering and did not know how to stop it. When it was revealed that he had a wife and child, I intuitively knew that she must have been pregnant. He had the integrity to marry her. This reminded me of the situation I was born into.

When I listened to my first Beatle album, I did not know whose voice was whose. I was lying on the sofa and there were three songs in a row by the same vocalist. At the end of the third song, *All I've Gotta Do*, I had my first little spontaneous orgasm. No touch involved, just the swirling of energy within. I remember slowly reaching over to the table next to me and picking up the album to see who was singing those songs. John! Oh, John again.

People were unapproachable. No one shared anything personal, not even family or friends. Even John's early songs like *I'm a Loser, Nowhere Man and Help* were revealing how he was feeling. No one in my life was telling me anything about themselves. But John was, this man spinning around on a record.

Lennon always had an edge. I remember one of the first books released about the Beatles, *The Beatles Forever* by Nicholas Schafner described each Beatle as they entered our experience and what type of girl would go for them. "For girls with intellectual, precocious or rebellious inclinations, John Lennon was the Beatle."

I believe that I understood John and recognized his vulnerability and honesty. Unlike many rockers, I felt the hard guy rock and roll persona was a thin veneer and underneath was a man of great depth, wisdom and concern for the world. I always said John Lennon was a rock star like Jesus was a carpenter. People usually did not understand why he was doing what he was doing. But whatever he did, I always absolutely understood his intention. He was the first person who made any sense to me. And few have since.

John and God

This is not about an obsession with a man; this is about a transformation of consciousness, his, mine and the world's.

When I was younger I was teased mercilessly about my love of John Lennon. But what was I saying? What did I mean and what do I mean when I say I love John Lennon. What am I saying, what am I loving? I am loving the belief that no matter how much suffering and pain there is in my life and the world I choose joy and love over and over again as my basis for reality, the place I intend to live my life from, the place I believe life can be about for all of us, what it's meant to be, what we are all working towards as we realize God within us. The music that he began and that he and his soul brothers created is pure celebration of life, full of energy and hope, a real feel good experience, releasing the mind and body from the deepest depression, inspiring us to what is so great about being alive! Singing, singing our song to the world, dancing, moving the body that God gave us till we feel ecstasy and jubilation. This is what I feel when I listen to the Beatles.

Life is to be enjoyed! What a revelation! What a revolution!

Loving John Lennon means offering myself to God for my consciousness to be completely transformed, to grow past much of my fears and lower emotions. It's to work from a personality full of conflict to one of peace. It's overcoming overpowering jealousy, doing everything I need to do to change myself so

I can experience a respect filled and loving relationship. It's becoming a personal conduit to relieve suffering in the world. It's in choosing to remove every form of violence from my life, and hopefully contributing to peace on the planet.

One really big surprise for me when John died was how the world reacted. As much as I, since the age of eleven was running around so excited about this man, saying to people, did you hear what he said? Did you get the meaning of those lyrics? Wow! This guy is incredible; he is what it's all about! This guy is really feeding us. I found myself saying years later before I made the connection that Lennon was like mother's milk, he fed me the real stuff, no fluff, just truth and hope and how to get there.

Everyone laughed at me or totally rejected me and then he died and the world went nuts mourning him. For me it was "damn, you all really do know what's really important! You really do know who he is and what he's talking about. But it took this for you all to admit it! Why? Why?" I still don't have the answer to that question.

Lennon to me played the part of mother- father- brother- lover, he was a true Guru.

How did he transform me? He was here to point the way, to go first, to show us what to do, not to be idolized and then ignored. There's a really big difference.

For me, Lennon's power was in his amazing ability to reveal himself in all his screwed - upness while relentlessly working to make himself a better person. This is what makes him effective. We can look at him in all our woundedness, see that he was wounded too, but yet he could do all that he did with his life. Well, I can at least do something with mine. This was key to my connection to him and how I was able to receive from his writing and life to overcome my childhood situation and create a life worth living. Hopefully, I will at least sometime in some way contribute to a better world.

When he said: "Now that I've showed you what I been through, don't take nobody's word for what you can do." It was a call to life, to believe in myself to move from almost total annihilation from being told I was nothing and I was worthless and not capable of anything. My father's favorite word for anyone was <u>idiot</u>. Whenever I wanted to do or be anything my mother would tell me that's not for us, we're the working bees. *Working Class Hero* put me on my knees literally thanking God that John was truly everything I ever thought he was with the depth of my pain and experience being expressed in that song. This is true for so many of us. And offering hope, a way out, and follow him, I did, I'm out!!!!!! I often expressed my childhood as being lost on a desert island with two things, cats and the Beatles. My cats kept my love alive, the Beatles, my ticket out or maybe better said my "ticket to ride."

As much of a Beatles fan that I am, I have always been up against an inner voice telling me that I am pathetic. That the original reason I connected with them was because I didn't have a life, that my life was so empty and devoid of meaning that I latched on to them out of great need. Au contraire. Maybe I came here just because of them to be on the planet when they were here, to join the fun and to be spiritually transformed to a better person through their message and teachings. Maybe, thank god, my life wasn't full of other distractions so I could

WHEN LIFE SENDS YOU LEMONS, MAKE LENNONAID

give myself over completely to the experience of the Beatles. To this day the ripple of the Beatles still is flowing out across the world. There is multi-generational enjoyment of their music and continuous releasing of more material. They are celebrated at the Fest for Beatle Fans and Beatle week in Liverpool and other conventions around the world. There is a wonderful presentation called Deconstructing the Beatles touring the country with detailed information on how the great songs were created, a course at Yale about the Beatles and a Master's Degree in Beatles. There are countless Beatle Brunches, though I can't imagine any could be more fun for me then Philadelphia's Andre Gardner with his enthusiasm, expertise and his road trips. He sometimes broadcasts his show from restaurants and from a beautiful boat floating down a river. And thankfully Paul and Ringo are still touring.

In a book by Cynthia, she tells of John whacking her across the face with jealousy. May Pang told of him throwing her across the room. John told us he hit women. John could be deplorable. Like Bono said: "John Lennon already told us he was an asshole, no one else has to do it for him." I do believe that a lot of John's public actions for peace from a psychological perspective could be seen as projections of his own inner world, as he so desperately searched for peace within himself. Our internal and external worlds are always bouncing back and forth. John wanted peace for the world as well as himself, which pretty much reflects the human condition, something we all need so badly.

Once again we see why he is so loved, even with his sometimes bad behavior. This is such the point. All my life people have been concerned that I am someone naive or foolish in admiring him so much. That he was this sweet saint or something, quite contrary and that's where his personal power to touch people (me) arises from. Lennon's story is one of transformation and intention. He wanted to be a loving person. He struggled with such anger and violence within himself, revealing his struggle to the world, and we see our own realness and struggle reflected back. A preacher who professes to have found God and is perfect and wants to help the rest of us fools find our way doesn't help. I can't relate, I'm not like them, I'm like John, struggling with my own ego and personality but oh, how I want to be that loving person. My life is dedicated to cleaning out as much of myself as I can to be that person. I believe John eventually turned into a person with that intention too. I believe his last five years were his most important for himself, when he turned inward and really did the personal work to put his walk and talk together, like we all must do. I feel his last five years were his personal sadhana, his spiritual work, when he really looked in the mirror and stopped playing out his need for attention, approval and projection onto the world's stage. Both were needed, we needed him to play out in the big arena to help us and then he needed to get quiet and personal to really help make peace himself.

My Relationship with God

Transforming my relationship with God is one of the biggest things I have to thank John Lennon for. I learned to question the religion I was brought up with and eventually make inner contact with a God that is a guide and friend rather than one that judges and punishes. My parents came from Christian Protestant backgrounds. The first few years of my life were lived in a city. We moved to a suburb shortly before my 4th birthday. My father did not have his license due to a DUI and accident so we walked everywhere. The closest church was a fundamentalist Baptist so off I went. My father never went to church (getting him there became a quest of my young life and I got him there once I think!). My mother went occasionally but I got shipped off every week for Sunday school, vacation Bible School in the summer and Pioneer Girls during the week (Christian Girl Scouts).

I've got to tell you my biggest response was "Where's the love?" I can pretty safely say I don't remember any friendliness, kindness or companionship from anyone I met there. This was a group of pretty uptight, unhappy folks. The rules and regulations of behavior took the fun out of anything life may have had to offer. There was harsh judgment against anyone but those who followed all the rules and saw life exactly the same. Those that didn't admit they were a rotten sinner and ask Jesus Christ into their Heart (this is the born again part) were truly going to burn in hell for eternity. This included all the poor fools who never heard of Jesus Christ, thus all the missionaries in Africa, one of which I wanted to be. Unfortunately I started my missionary on a young Catholic friend. I still remember trying to get up my nerve to give her the bad news that she had to do this thing, admit she was a sinner and let Jesus into her heart in this certain way (the Catholics weren't doing it right) or I really believed she would suffer in this hideous way for time ever after. I so wanted to save her but she must have told her mother of our conversation because I never saw her again.

At the church, I remember being yanked out of a chair and being dragged to a different one when I sat where I wasn't supposed to. I remember overhearing very young adolescent girls, this is early sixties mind you, talking of nothing but the sex they were having, and saying really mean things about everyone they knew including each other. I remember it being a sin to dance! A sin to dance, a sin to celebrate life and body, the one thing I naturally did well and LOVED to do. My mother was rejected by the other women of the church because she smoked cigarettes. Then she kept trying to stop drinking because that was a sin too, of course. I remember my mother showing up at a family party with a bottle of ginger ale with a homemade label saying Baptist Champagne. I had this beautiful picture of Jesus on the wall in my room, a decoupage on a slice of tree where he is holding a sheep that is looking at him with such love, the flock of sheep walking with him, looking up all bliss- eyed. Jesus was so soft and gentle; he seemed to offer such comfort and peace. I wasn't getting any of that in "his" church. Where's the love?

Enter the Beatles, I'm feeling love now. I'm feeling real joy, I'm jumping up and down, I'm singing, I'm DANCING I'm shaking my head and screaming! Oh my god, this music makes me feel wonderful! I'm energized like never before in my life, I may even get off the sofa. This is a call to wake up, a call to life, and a call to participate. This has got the juice, this is the real deal, there is really something happening here, this has the spark, the light, this is happy music, I feel it Lord, I feel it.

And the day came, John's infamous words: "Christianity will go," it will vanish and shrink. I needn't argue with that—I'm right and I will be proved right. We're more popular than Jesus now; I don't know which will go first, rock n roll or Christianity. Jesus was right but his disciples were thick and ordinary. It's them twisting it that ruins it for me." Whoa!

That summed it up for me. You need to understand this started a questioning, a soul searching that lasted maybe 40 years to bring me fully back to Jesus but in a pure sense. I don't believe that Jesus would be a Christian. The church has little to do with the message or meaning of Jesus. That the basis even starts with the only way to God and heaven is Jesus? It immediately contradicts Jesus' message of tolerance and equality. He doesn't need to be the only one, or the best one or the top one. This is simply another construct of the human ego.

I was a young girl of 13. Earlier that year, my mother had handed me a page from the Sunday paper that in the upper right hand corner had a little ad, maybe 3 inches by two inches, The Beatles were coming to our town. She sent a check for FIVE bucks (do you know what I just paid for McCartney tickets?) My mother did this for me and I held a little ticket in my hand that said 8th row. Wow!!!

So as the summer tour approaches, John Lennon opens his big mouth (thank god, no pun intended!) and the tour may be cancelled! Everywhere I am hearing what a bad man John Lennon is, how could he say such a terrible thing!!!!

So I attempted to do what I was supposed to do as a good little Christian girl. The walls and doors of my tiny bedroom were of course, covered in Beatle posters along with a beautiful box I had decorated to keep John's book in (notice, not the Bible). I remember so clearly putting my desk chair up against the closet door, climbing up to take the posters down. And then I stopped midair, tack in hand and thought to myself, "he's right" and then and there I choose to follow John Lennon, not the Jesus that the church had presented to me. And through John Lennon I learned in the real living sense, the teachings of Jesus

Christ and eventually gained a flourishing relationship with the genuine Christ, one that offers true unconditional love and helps my soul to grow towards love and peace. John Lennon took me to the real religion, the real God, the real Christ. And I learned about Buddha and Krishna and a few others along the way and they all helped me feel better about myself and my life.

WAR IS OVER IF YOU WANT IT

John and Yoko placed the words WAR IS OVER IF YOU WANT IT on billboards and full page newspaper ads around the world. This was one of the most amazing things I ever saw growing up. Are you kidding? That someone with all this fame and money would take the time and use their resources to utilize the media for this? To use this form of communication for some other reason than to convince us that we need something so they can sell it to us? I'm jumping up and down with the excitement of it all, the cleverness, the whole idea of using mass communication to wake us up! Think! Wake up! The powers in your hands! Good news! WAR IS OVER! Dancing in the streets! We're free! We can enjoy life! Love each other! Grow together! Have a ball!

From the Medicine House News, Christmas Eve, 1969: "Most Canadians cannot help but react with skepticism to Lennon's current crusade. His goal of world peace is an admirable one, of course, but his methods of realizing his ideal are naive. And to end war between nations-to official violence-cannot be achieved by buying full page ads in the New York Times or by bleating 'Give Peace a Chance' in the streets of Toronto. These are exercises in futility. Theatrics that don't resolve anything. Every sane person on Earth wants peace, but most of us are sophisticated enough to know that only our leaders can end war."

John and Yoko are really trying to tell us what's real. It is all so opposite of what everyone has been convinced to believe. The world full of hate and war is the illusion because we believe it's the only way it can be. We've been tricked. It is not real, albeit the illusion is so strong it may well destroy us all but it is not the truth. Love really is the only truth, no matter how lost most of us may be.

I can guarantee you this. If you believe that John & Yoko were naive or unsophisticated then I promise you, you are still asleep. You have not awoken. You are still hypnotized. They still got you. You are still under the illusion and brainwashed.

I realized one of the most spirit- killing comments that people can make about John Lennon and Yoko Ono (and me) is that the work they did on behalf of peace is naive. I have in the past been intimidated by this, felt disempowered and embarrassed about myself for feeling the same way and loving and believing in John Lennon so much.

I can no longer be made to feel that way or be convinced that he was naive or that I am. When someone says that, I can now see that they are likely just showing me how closed they are. John Lennon wasn't naive He was living a truth that most people still cannot see. He lived at a high level of truth and truth is simple, not naive.

Should we be leaving peace up to world leaders to create? World leaders are the last people who want peace. You think they care how many peasants (that's us folks) die? It's about weapon building contracts, rebuilding contracts, and oil profits.

So many years later the world is still talking about what John and Yoko did. Their events touched the imagination and the heart. Their message has been quietly working inside to help people awaken and change. What will save the earth is a change of heart within each and every one of us. John and Yoko started a big wave that is still reverberating through humanity. When our hearts change, everything will fall into place. If you don't believe me, then know yours is yet to open.

When we are taught history in our schools we are being taught HisStory of War. The study of history is the chauvinistic assumption that the only thing that's happened in humanity's story worth noting is war. Any other subject is given the title "the history of such and such" but when you see just the world history, we all know what's coming; the story of conquest, violence and rape. It is the indoctrination and brainwashing of us into the belief that humans are defined by the wars they wage. There is a conscious emphasis that perpetuates the mindset that keeps wars going.

We are so steeped in the illusion that war is inevitable, being an innate part of life on this planet that we don't even see that we are creating it, that we are choosing it.

Therefore we can, create something else, and choose something else. If we put our attention to it, it's all we see. We could focus on the positive, surface it and bring it forth. The positive is happening parallel to the negative, right next to it, so if we could just shift our perception just a little....if we want to. I must admit I am often surprised, hurt and frustrated by how many people will tell me they want peace on earth but yet submerge themselves in the violence often found on TV, movies and books. On a personal level they are still getting off on it, stuck in the mire, falling to the lowest common denominator. It's feeding the monster within on a personal level. Please let's try to lift ourselves up. Surround yourself with what is higher and you easily stimulate that part of yourself. By watching this stuff and even paying for our own indoctrination, our own depression, our own defeatism, we are continuing to keeping ourselves asleep.

The world isn't just the way it is because that's the way it is. WE are creating it this way, we are choosing it and we can create and choose something else like a world where WAR IS OVER if we want it.

Everybody's talkin' bout.....

Bagism.......which was the idea of John and Yoko's for people to present themselves to others, especially prospective employers completely covered by a black bag. This would help eliminate the usual prejudices associated with race, skin color, rich, poor, old, young, religion, etc. A person could be given a better chance if they could present their character and capabilities without being judged by all the assumptions made by one's appearance. It was a good starting point to start to chip away at all the ways we judge each other every day when we just look at each other.

Recently on Facebook there was a video of a screen with people gathered around it on the street. What you see are skeletons hugging and when they come around the front and reveal themselves you see many different types of people; gays, heterosexuals, old, young, every kind of color, race and religion. The skeletons all look the same. We are still learning these lessons that John and Yoko so creatively presented to us.

John Lennon's Defenses

The contrast between Lennon's outward cruelty and his inner vulnerability touches me to the core. When I read the lyrics of songs like *How, Mother, Working Class Hero, Julia, Help, I'm a Loser*, etc., the depth this man is able to go to inside and create art with it and then to have lived in the world of rock n roll must have been an insurmountable challenge. This man was capable of leaving his heart, soul and body bare (Two Virgins album cover) to the human race and winds it into a blaring electric guitar. And we poured our pain and neediness back at him. How could he hold up under it all? "Lick my lingam" is a line from The Two of Us a movie about an imagined day of conversation between John and Paul in 1976. Adoring people approach him fawning and he throws out his mean words to protect himself from feeling their desperate needs and his own. Lennon was a one-off, one of a kind, no other soul was willing to expose himself at this level of soul communication and touch so many people. His hard callous shell was not a contradiction, it was a survival mechanism. If John Lennon ever read this writing, would he thank me or tell me to lick his lingam?

MORE SONG LYRICS (WHAT THEY MEANT TO ME)

These songs contain words of wisdom and teachings. I can only use 8 lines from each song. I heartily suggest you look up the full lyrics on the internet.

I'll Cry Instead

When did John Lennon start to reveal himself in his lyrics? It starts with *I'll Cry Instead*, in my opinion. "I've got every reason on earth to be mad" (which he is, very mad) "cause I've just lost the only girl I've had" (mother) "If I could see her now" (he speaks knowing that he can't because she's passed on) "I'd try to make her sad somehow, but I can't so I'll cry instead" (so he makes all the women in his life sad). It would have done him good to cry but he does everything else but cry; he drinks, drugs, fights, womanizes, and beats up his girlfriends. He does everything to not cry but somehow he knows that crying should be involved in his feelings and actions. Jump ahead to primal therapy when he says. "Primal therapy allowed us to feel feelings continually, and those feelings usually make you cry." "I've got a chip on my shoulder bigger then my feet" (people who knew Lennon in his younger days have said just this) "I can't talk to people that I meet" (so he shows scorn).

And when he says: "I'm gonna break their hearts all around the world," he's not kidding. How many loved and idolized and wanted him? Still! New ones every generation! This is a man mad at his mama and not only did his girlfriends and wives pay with cheating and violence and meanness but women all around the world who never met him pined for his love. This guy is powerful even is his negativity. Thank god he worked to change his purpose to spreading love and peace and utilized his immense personal power for good

The Word

As a young child I loved Jesus and had a good relationship with him. I remember I would often meet him in a cloud and talk with him about life looking down at earth. I had a beautiful slice of a tree trunk decoupage with a picture of Jesus walking while holding a lamb as other sheep gathered around his feet looked up at him adoringly. I would look at the gentleness of love that Jesus shone on the little lamb and love this man and his kindness. That little plaque is one of the few mementos of childhood I kept except for my Beatle memorabilia. I even still love sheep. Going to church is what ruined it for me with Jesus.

Luckily there was for me a genuine experience of love and joy that religion talks about available for me in the world. The Beatles. They have kept me and my love alive. I know it's a path that works for me, has given me what I need, even me back to myself.

I believe that John is speaking of God in the song *The Word*. Obviously, John Lennon is speaking beyond romantic love to spiritual love, the love from the divine.

First John tells us to "say the word and you'll be free", find real love, the love streaming from the source and you will be free of all the strife and struggle being stuck in the mire that earth brings to us, "say the word and be like me", a self-actualized person living at their creative potential carrying the message of God's love and oneness. He tells us that spiritual love is "so fine, it's sunshine." It's all that feels good; it's illumination as you look around this world.

He talks of misunderstanding the word in the beginning but now he knows "the word is good." Like so many, he laughed and scoffed at such things when he was young but now he understands it is the purpose of life, to connect with, to feel and to spread the light of God's love in a real way, not how it has been polluted by religions.

"Now I know what I feel must be right, I'm here to show everybody the light" begins Lennon's conscious spiritual awareness. He is announcing his purpose and intention as a teacher to humanity of love and peace.

For me, when I am referring to God, I am referring to the source, the benevolent energy creating the universe. I see no argument between creationism and evolution. Evolution is God creating. When someone tells me they are an atheist I wonder if it is really religion they do not believe in. For me, if something exists, like the universe, something had to create it. And that creator source is God. By definition if something exists, something created it and that I call God.

Julia

Learning to play piano turned out to be mainly another way to experience Beatle music. Playing the songs for myself takes feeling the music another level deeper. Playing some of my favorites for the first time brought me to tears, *And I Love Her,*

Here there and Everywhere, Imagine. When I linger over the notes I feel each note deep inside. It is breathtaking.

The sadness expressed when I hear the song *Julia* barely relates to the depth I feel it when I play it. Each run through takes me deeper inside, hearing and feeling the sadness that feels exquisite actually. It's a sweet sadness, the blending of love and loss and the hope through the lines dedicated to Yoko. Sadness can be exquisite as it takes us to the still place inside if we let it. It centers us, takes us to the place where we touch each other and connect. Right now I am looking at John's picture and feel totally with him. I love the beauty of him once he could express his feelings through sadness rather than anger and rebellion. God bless his transforming soul.

Dear Prudence

If anyone was to ask me what my personal favorite Beatle song is I would answer with this one. The song is full of light and promise of a better day and I believed him. The words answered such a personal need in me, touched my sadness and gave me hope.

"Won't you come out to play" was an invitation to me to join life, I could stop hiding away on the sofa. He sang of the beautiful healing aspects of nature, the sun, the blue sky, and the singing birds and reminded me that I was part of it too. And just to contemplate that the line about being beautiful could apply to me as well. I enjoy the way the song builds to that wonderful cymbal crash and then poignantly fades out. I always particularly noticed how superb the drumming is on this song, I was surprised to find out it was Paul! I love Ringo's drumming but Paul does a fine job on this song.

I am the Walrus

"I am he as you are he as you are me and we are all together."
Oneness, we all come from the same source, we are all connected
on a higher level and we are all on this planet together. The
sooner we get this, the better.

All You Need is Love

For me this song is about universal love, the path of love,
illumination, and living life from a centered place when we
connect with the energy of God within us. Then everything
in our life falls into place and begins to flow. "There's nowhere
you can be that isn't where you're meant to be." All is shown,
all is known, and everyone is saved

Instant Karma

This song is significant because of its time and place. The song
was coming out of an AM radio speaking in a very clever and
poetic style of deep spiritual truths. Since then, through so
many spiritual teachers, this information has come to light,
but this is where I first heard it. The ideas were new, different
than what I had been brought up to believe. Yet it rang true
as soon as I heard it, made sense and changed me....instantly.....

First Lennon speaks of how life will knock you right on the
head if you're not listening to what you need to hear when it
whispers. Then John reminds us that our life in finite and we
only have a limited amount of time to grow as souls in this
incarnation, to open our hearts to ourselves and other people.

"What in the world are you thinking of laughing in the face of love?" I hear him talking to himself in his hard cold cruel past as he awakens to softness and letting women and God's love in, as well as for all of us. We choose so much other than love for so long – like sex and clothes and drugs and food and fame and fancy cars and TV and watching movies and competition with each other over anything and video games and anything else this world offers up until we can feel what we really need. We realize what we need is love in its godly sense, kindness, compassion, taking care of ourselves and each other, sharing, giving, gratefulness, appreciation of the beauty of nature, of animals, and forgiveness. How people actually do laugh at those of us who care for such things as foolish and simplistic and idealistic, there is money to be made and things to have and that is all there is. This is a really poignant description of what we are doing until we can finally start to feel what we really need. This is not false fleeting romantic love that people actually think is the love he's talking about. What is meant is spiritual love, the kind that makes us care about all living beings. John tells us it's up to each and everyone one of us.

"Why on earth are we here, surely not to live in pain and fear?" This speaks deeply to me of my own childhood and life, certainly, but once again I feel he speaks to humanity's bigger questions. Surely there is enough resources at the most basic level so that we can all be taken care of and live our lives in pursuit of greater and greater creative output. We can be discovering deeper spiritual truths and having great feeling internal spiritual energy experiences. Our lives can be glorious expressions of divinity. We need not be suffering in pain in all its forms both physical and emotional. We need not live in fear of harm, starvation and lack of love.

Lennon tells us humanity needs to see each other as equal and worthy of the earth's resources. We need to realize the oneness that the spiritual teachers speak of. We can then treat each other with respect and nonviolence. We would no longer judge by the ways we do of sex, race, color, and religion. We would value each other as another human being as worthy of a good life, as ourselves.

"Why on earth are you there, when you're everywhere, come and get your share." This spoke to me personally, these are some of the lines that helped me believe I did deserve something better in life. Why are you so stuck in your sadness and unworthiness when your consciousness is everywhere, anywhere, and unlimited. You can have and be what you want in life, we all can, open your mind, let go of what you were taught to believe about life and yourself, this is what is true, it's all here for you. Everyone has a share.

"We all shine on." There is no death as we think of it; we are all immortal beautiful spirits that shine with God's love forever.

I Found Out

The lyrics to *I found out* were one of the more personal and helpful songs for me. First John talks about what he's been through, all that he had to overcome but still achieved. He tells us this is true for all of us. Don't let anyone else tell you what you can accomplish in this life. This epitomizes my struggle throughout life and even now. My childhood experiences left me feeling powerless, that I could not accomplish anything in the world. John is telling me that this is not true, not to give up, that he went through so much as a child but yet was able to express himself creatively and show up on the world's stage and contribute.

When he talks about "there ain't no Jesus gonna come from the sky, now that I found out I know I can cry." This really spoke to me having been brought up as a fundamentalist Christian and being taught that Jesus was going to come and save the good people. I realized this is a Christian myth and I was able to understand there was no magic solution to my pain and suffering and I could feel the sadness of that.

When he talks about men with "their cock in their hand, don't get you nowhere, don't make you a man," I believe this talks to our seemingly endless focus on sex rather than love and relationship, the perpetual scoring that somehow is supposed to increase your status and worth as a man but it gets you nowhere, it's not what anyone really needs.

John talks about his parents not wanting him, which led to his obsession to be massive in the music business. Simplistic in some ways but true that the lack of his real mother and any mothering feeling from Mimi who was hard and cruel could have put a neurotic need in him for continuous love and approval that translated to the stage and its adoration and applause.

He speaks of our generation's new religious hopes when we turned to the east but found them disappointing as well, "there ain't no Guru who can see through your eyes." Having spent time at an ashram and my guru falling from grace for the usual sexual improprieties, I found that out too.

John also took a clever jab at Paul with his reference to

"seeing religion from Jesus to Paul." I believe he is definitely not referring to Paul of Damascus but to Paul McCartney's tendency to be overbearing at the end of the Beatles.

Then he talks of "not being fooled by dope and cocaine, no one can harm you, feel your own pain." This is definitive as he sees through the illusion of drugs and learns that feeling one's emotions are the only way through and out of our psychological pain and suffering.

How?

This is a song that I feel expresses how I and likely many others feel inside. And put so poetically and beautifully. "How can I go forward when I don't know which way I am facing?" That expresses so well my early feelings of being lost in life, not knowing what I am doing, I want my life to get better but where am I, how do I it, what direction will help me? I don't know how.

John speaks of having had feelings denied for so long, having not been able to feel for so long he doesn't even "know if something is a feeling." This so describes how removed we end up from our true self trying to please everyone, fit in, behave, make do, make no waves, cooperate, and hide our hurts.

John shares with us that he wants to give love but he doesn't even know what it is, he doesn't know how to give it because he has never had any. Isn't that true for so many of us? And I don't mean what passes for love even in the best of families, which is still so superficial and conditional that it doesn't reach our soul and comfort us, doesn't provide us a real sense of self-worth.

How can I tell you how deeply this song helped me not feel so alone with these same feelings so beautifully expressed? How can I tell you how deeply I needed this man and his message? How can I express how much this song meant to me? How deeply it touched me, how much I felt from hearing it, how it helped me to feel what he talks about in this song. How grateful I am to John Lennon for it.

You Can't Do That/Run for Your Life/Jealous Guy

This is an amazing progression of emotional growth and self-awareness. We start out with young John with *You Can't Do That* concerned only for himself, his feelings and how he looks to others. He's going to cause her pain by dropping her if he sees her talking to another guy again. His ego is much invested, everyone is jealous because he has this girl but he is concerned that people will laugh at him if she talks to someone else. He at least has the awareness to share that he: "can't help my feelings, I go out of my mind." This song is rough, possessive and I question if there is really any caring or love for the girl.

Next we move onto *Run for Your Life*. His jealousy is totally out of control as he is now threatening a woman's life. He would rather see her "dead then to be with another guy." He calls himself wicked and refers to his jealous mind. Lennon himself later said he didn't like this song. And of course we know who the cheater was. Lennon was notorious for his cheating. Good old psychological mirroring and projection.

But after Lennon gets older and I would say after the effect of Primal Therapy we find a new John who now can own his jealous feelings and his pain and even has concern for their effect on his partner. *Jealous Guy* begins with acknowledging his mind has gone to the past (his mother ultimately? Julia has a new man and John goes to Aunt Mimi?) He begins to lose control of his emotions. He admits insecurity and his fear that he might not be loved anymore. He knows and can feel how his behavior has hurt another and he is apologizing. At the end he can't resist just a little threat with his "watch out baby" but he has come a long way. This song is a miracle in the psychological growth that it reveals Lennon has reached at this time. It is also a masterpiece and exquisite in its expression of truth in describing the emotion of jealousy, one that I know very well and so do most of us.

Woman is the Nigger of the World

This song took guts for any man to sing let alone a rock and roller. The lyrics truthfully describe women's experience. The lyrics speak for themselves. I love the line "If you don't believe me take a look at the one you're with." Again, this reveals his ability to communicate directly to us as if he knows us personally and we are having a conversation. He always puts his teachings into experience not just intellectual statements. It also includes his call to action. "Do something about it." Yoko taught him so much and he was willing to learn and he became a powerful spokesperson for the needed changes in our world. He came from Liverpool with traditional working class definitions of women and their role in society. To be able to transform himself into someone who could understand a woman's pain and proclaim it to the world made him an admirable man.

Every line in this song is an insight into women's experience. Standing out the most for me: "We make her bear and raise our children and then leave her flat for being a fat old mother hen.

We tell her home is the only place she should be, and then we complain she is too unworldly to be our friend.

We insult her everyday on TV then wonder why she has no guts or confidence."

This was script perfect for my mother's day and still holds credence today, though more subtle.

A woman's worth is dismissed and taken from her through our culture. She is dumbed down to her own capabilities and the worst double trick of all; after raising children, left for someone younger whose body and face does not show the wear and tear of doing this for years. This is certainly the world my mother grew up in and my generation intended to bust wide open. It did in some ways but seems to have gotten usurped by the ego.

Mind Games/Walls & Bridges/Rock and Roll

I clearly remember when I bought the Mind Games album I put it on the turntable and listened from start to finish. I put it back in the sleeve and album and quietly sat down and felt that something was wrong. I looked at the cover photo and saw Yoko as huge as a mountain and a very small John. Was he walking away? He seemed to be implying how huge she was to him but yet......I soon found out they had separated.

I felt this deeply. They had been such a model for me of what I wanted in a relationship. John had been so demonstrative about how much he valued and loved this woman. He allowed her to teach him so much about what it was like to be a woman in this society transforming him from a classic "chauvinistic pig" to a true advocate for women's rights. They were such a glorious team working so originally and creatively for world peace.

They couldn't keep it together? We know now that the worst part of John had broken them up, the infamous night of the Nixon win when he cheated on her in the next room for all attending to hear. This feels to me like one of the worst public humiliations of all time. And for all she had given him. What had he really learned?

Off he went on this lost weekend with their assistant May Pang. Yoko was still loving him, sending him off with another woman to look after him. It became his last stand of debauchery at its finest.

The songs on the album reflect higher consciousness and his love for Yoko. I love *Mind Games*. He says so much beautifully and poetically about humankind's evolution towards peace, love and understanding. This is our goal. I love the lines "projecting our images in space and in time," it reminded me of when he appeared astrally in the cab outside Madison Square Garden. *Intuition* follows a similar theme of confirming that we know how to live life when we live it from the inside, trusting our instincts in the form of the inner voice that prompts us and guides us in our lives..

During John and Yoko's time apart he created the album with the brilliant title *Walls and Bridges*. I imagine this spoke to his mental state at the time, he certainly created walls around his psyche and heart with his alcohol and drug use but being John there were still bridges to reach him and for him to reach out and touch us.

Songs address the break up. *Going Down on Love:* "when the real thing goes wrong and you can't get it on." "Something precious and rare disappears in thin air" "Well you know, the price is right!" Higher reaching, love preaching John is gone...."shoot out the light, ain't coming home for the night." "Sow your wild oats." We find more of the same on *What You Got* with "It's Saturday night and I just gotta rip it up. Sunday morning I just got to give it up."

And John's only #1 hit after the Beatles: *Whatever gets you through the Night* where he in very few words throws away all he has tried to teach over the years. The title says it all, do whatever it takes to make it through the night, "do it wrong or do it right" just drink, drug, womanize, whatever it takes to not feel the pain of life. This song went over big. This, the world could relate to. He at least does have the line "whatever ever gets you to the light" so he hasn't forgotten everything...

Scared for me on the album was a masterpiece of Lennon's courage and soul revealing honesty. Again, saying what most men would not by simply saying: "I'm scared." He speaks of "no bell, book or candle can get you out of this" as "the straws slip away." John is untethered, so very much alone and lost and all his psychological and spiritual work cannot take away his overwhelming fear.

He speaks so well of being overcome by the lower emotions: "Hatred and jealousy gonna be the death of me, I guess I knew it right from the start. Sing out about love and peace; don't wanna see the red raw meat. The green eyed goddamn straight from your heart." Guts! Who else could be so honest with himself and share it with us all? How deeply I share those same contradictory feelings; how connected I feel to him because he told me he feels that way too. And I was scared at that time in my life as well. I was mostly alone, taking care of my sick and crazy parents, working my way through college, dealing with my own addictions, not knowing if I would ever find love and create a happy life.

Nobody Loves You finds a world weary John who has seen it all, "seen the one eyed witch doctor leading the blind" who has tried everything to transform himself into a better person and create a happy life but "every time I put my finger on it, it slips away."

He speaks directly to us, using his ability to communicate with us so personally: "I've been across to the other side, I've shown you everything, I've got nothing to hide, but still you ask me do I love you, all I can tell you is it's all showbiz." He tells us he has given us all he is, his fans, humanity and yet we still wonder if he cares for us. And the ultimate irony line, "it's all showbiz," he being the one person who so rose above "show biz" to use it as a vehicle of communication for soul truths and spiritual enlightenment.

At the end of *I'm Scared*, John tells us how tired he is. I think this is a clue as to what is coming. When he does go back to Yoko, he leaves us for a while and takes a five year sabbatical from show biz.

The Rock and Roll album certainly brought everything full circle for John. There was more hell in some ways with Phil Spector producing and all his violent shenanigans and the tapes disappearing and the lawsuit with Levy. His performance of *Be-Bop A-Lula* is perfection, no one could beat it. But his most personal statement comes at the end of the record where he tells us "this is Dr. Winston O' Boogie saying goodnight from record Plant East New York, we hope you had a swell time, everybody here says hi....goodbye." He does not record any more music for five years.

Lennon returns with Yoko with the *Double Fantasy* album. His fabulous rock n roll song *Starting Over* hits it out of the ballpark, his voice is so strong and the power of the song builds to a screaming peak. Again, we find heartfelt honesty from both John and Yoko about their relationship as well as the beautiful song written for Sean and the sincere tribute to Yoko. They had come full circle.

Watching the Wheels

I believe this song was a foreshadowing of what was soon to come. As much as the song is a brilliant description of Lennon's house-husband days and his growing past the pop music business put so poetically, it also speaks to watching the world from the other side, from death. When he says at the end so poignantly...."I just had to let it go" he was telling us he needed to let this life go.......

Working Class Hero

This song literally put me on my knees the first time I heard it. It nailed my experience and the pain from it perfectly in life. And it bonded me to John Lennon a zillion times more deeply. This proved to me that I had been right all along in who I thought he was and what he was capable of being and doing.

Often I hear people say when they refer to this song that Lennon was brought up in a nice house so this invalidates the working class hero claim. Anyone who had to grow up and work and therefore is molded and prepared for it from the time they are born is included in this song. And that speaks to most of us; we are "given no time instead of it all." We are not given an opportunity to find out who we are, explore our creative potential, find out what we want to do. Our lives are dictated to us through whatever level of work we are born into, from the lowest people who know that they will never go to college and will struggle with some back- breaking manual labor position - to the upper working classes who are forced by status and prestige into some soul numbing profession based on making large amounts of money no matter the cost to personal freedom, other humans, animals or the earth itself.

John begins the song with the line: "as soon as you're born they make you feel small." This spoke to me on a deeply personal level. My mother was always telling me we were the "worker bees" and I could not have the art, dance lessons or piano lessons that I so wanted. I had so much creativity inside of me that was crushed and thwarted. I realize now not having the money was a big part of it but that's not how she put it. I could have understood her perspective but I was made to feel unworthy and not good enough. I have had to deal with an inner voice that says: "I can't" my whole life.

"Until the pain is so big you feel nothing at all" I feel by the time our childhood learning is done we are far removed from our true selves and our true needs. As a result of the overwhelming pain, we shut down to survive and preserve what little of our soul is left available to us. We are told who we are and what we will do by a world that has shut down its heart and has become unkind. And when we close off from the pain and don't feel anything we can commit all kinds of acts against each other, other beings and the earth. We also shut down to the wonder and beauty of the earth, the fragility of our bodies and hearts and feelings and the unfathomable violence that pervades our planet can happen. What if when we were born we were treated gently and our natural talents and desires honored, encouraged and respected? And we lived in a world where we were all taking care of each other so that no one lived in need? That who we are and what we really wanted to do could be pursued without danger of not having enough to survive?

"They hurt you at home and they hit you at school." Again this speaks of life numbing experiences we continuously pass on from each generation to the next, being hurt emotionally and physically everywhere we turn. "Till you're so fucking crazy you can't follow their rules." Oh my god, we end up in such a state of terror, confusion and frustration, we begin to act out in all sorts of psychological dysfunction and perpetuate the violence. Look around us, look at ourselves.

"When they're tortured and scared you for twenty odd years, then they expect you to pick a career but you can't really function you're so full of fear." Dear God! John Lennon bless you for these words, this truth, and this sanity describing the insanity of it all. How many young people are out of their minds on drugs and alcohol? We are hurting so much by being literally tortured in my case and many others by our supposed caretakers, our parents and other family members, teachers and nuns and priests, frightened over and over again by those closest to us and the world in general around us. Then, the message is – ok, now function in this world, this society, just get a job or a career, go to it every day, make and spend your money. Then find someone, get married, have children and that's the end of it. Now shut up about it. Now we get to the punch line which had me jumping up and down when I heard it......and just how do we shut up about it?

We "are doped with religion and sex and TV." Religion that takes us away from true inner connection, and the experience of spirit where we feel ecstasy and love for ourselves and all of life. Religion is lost in fighting about whose god is real, people controlled by ritual and dogma so they never think a thought for themselves and live in unexamined hypocrisy, sex becomes stuck at a third grade level of infantile expression, an industry of mutual exploitation, without love or caring for the eventual fate of a sexual partner. And TV, turn it on when the day is done, just numb out to some inane passive brain draining "entertainment" so you can get up and do it again. "Well, you're still fucking peasants as far as I can see" is how John sees us. Oh I could weep for us all forever and a day. Where have we really gotten to? Most of us are out of little grass huts and literally being serfs, but how much power do we really have? How much freedom? Now we have all our entertainment without our souls, we don't have our hearts; we don't love ourselves or each other. Most of us are soul-sick and numbing ourselves whatever way we can to make it through another day and hopefully live to retirement so we can breathe a little freely before we die. At the end of the song, Lennon tells us that they teach us that if we want the good life too, we must learn to deceive, trick, manipulate, lie, and steal to really succeed in business. This is the way most of the world works if we want to be really rich and make so much money we can stop working and not be working class. Just sit back nice and fat and be among the top one percent taking the lion's share of the world's goods while we "kill" the rest of the earth's beings and the earth itself either literally or by not caring about what happens to them. He then asks us to follow him instead. I will and I did! You speak deep truth, dear soul John Lennon.

Imagine

Imagine is the song that is the companion of *Working Class Hero*. That song describes how it is; *Imagine* describes how it can be and what we are working to create at a deep soul level in the world.

Imagine is a world run by the power of love, not greed and it is as real a possibility as anything else. We have created the world as it is so we can create it differently as well. The song itself is a part of that process, it being heard and sung throughout the world for many years.

I know this song is seen as preposterous and hilarious to some considering the depth of greed and violence in this world. But with the switch of the heart this could all change in the blink of an eye or it could be gradual, starting with those who are already enlightened working its way through humanity until each soul is awakened. We know in classic religion in the conversion stories, the hardened criminal, the member of the mafia, the slave seller who has a change of heart and really gets what they have done and transforms to a loving person. This tells us the possibility is in each and every one of us that we could truly wake up and change and then we could live as one. Oneness is the world's message for we truly are connected under all the surface differences and ways of expressing our personalities and culture. For me the point is that something must truly awaken and change our hearts, no amount of policing or regulating or laws or social services or religion or parenting is going to do it. We just keep moving the pieces around on the game board but the game remains the same. We'll know it when it happens, we'll know it when it's real. Because we won't need to be policed or controlled, it'll truly be an inside job and we will just naturally treat each other with respect and kindness because that is all we know how to do. There will be no countries, no possessions, we will all share, why wouldn't we? There will be "nothing to kill or die for," we will all have what we need, and it's all here for us now.

Greed will disappear as we see all that we need is overflowing when we begin to share. Hunger gone forever, it's easy as pie to feed us all - there is enough food on the planet this very moment for everyone to eat. There are people who already know this, who already live like this, it's time we all joined them and the world will live as one.

When I first heard these words "you may say I'm the dreamer but I'm not the only one, I hope someday you'll join us and the world will be as one," John Lennon was the only other person beside myself that I knew that understood and believed this. The ache in my heart was so deep and I reached out to this soul to help me survive in a world where it seemed no one even considered such ideas. This is the importance of John Lennon for me, for so many years he was all I had to keep my dream alive of a better life for myself and for everyone. Since that time I have met, studied, read, worked, and lived with like-minded people who have dedicated their lives to spiritual growth to be able to live the ideals proclaimed in these lyrics. I am so grateful for all the risk and vulnerability John shared with the world to write music like this when "he could have just been playing for dances.*

Crazy John (1970)
(for John Lennon)
Words and Music by Tom Paxton

Crazy John, where you gonna run to today?
Crazy John, so early to be up and away,
They never can hear you, John, so how can you teach them?
They never come near you, John, so how can you reach them?

Crazy John, can I come along when you go?
Crazy John, you tell them what they don't want to know.
They never can hear you, John, they have no desire.
They're beginning to fear you, John, and the hate's getting higher.

When you wade in the water, the people can't see the old reflections.
When you stand in the road, the people can't read the old directions.
When the people get lost, they start building a cross.

Crazy John, why you wanna go back again?
Crazy John, talking with the desperate men
You have to be crazy, John, for taking those chances,
When you could be lazy, John, just playing for dances.

When you wade in the water, the people can't see the old reflections.
When you stand in the road, the people can't read the old directions.
When the people get lost, they start building a cross.

Crazy John, I want to be crazy too

---

* *Crazy John* by Tom Paxton

119

LOSING HIM

There is a book I had read many years earlier called *The Murder of Christ* by Wilhelm Reich. It was one of the most important books I ever read. It helped me understand human being's dynamics. Basically it says that Jesus was a lover of life and because of human's emotional armoring, most people cannot live their lives in the same open manner. Reich states that with Christ, or anyone who represents life truly being lived, at first they will be greatly admired. People believe simply by admiring someone, the qualities they want will somehow flow into them. When that doesn't happen, they turn on that person. Then the murder of Christ will take place. First people want to be with the person, hoping they will rub off on them. When that doesn't happen they become angry. Wilhelm Reich said that this person "will irrevocably be killed." At the time of my reading this book there was a statement that I underlined. "The murder has never yet failed to occur in the end." Beside that I had written: "Lennon Lives."

I remember at some time during the next day after John had been shot, I quietly walked over to my bookcase, opened the book to that page and wrote: "they killed John too."

For me, the events leading up to Lennon's death started in the summer of 1980. John had re-emerged. He had been away for five years, being a househusband, doing his sadhana, raising his and Yoko's son, and learning what it was like to be with himself - truly turning into the gentle person he had wanted to be. John and Yoko decided to make some music again. I believe they did most of the recording over the summer and released Double Fantasy in November 1980. I was so excited! My ex-husband called me when the first song released from the album, *Starting Over* was being played on the radio for the first time. He knew how much it would mean to me. The physical act of going out to buy Lennon's music again was exciting. John & Yoko looked great, a favorite joy in life had returned.

John was giving interviews, which he hadn't done in five years. I was going to hear what John had to say again. I'd find out how he had been transformed through taking care of his beautiful son. Everything was just going to be great again. My cosmic friend was back.

There was a short interview that appeared in the magazine, *Newsweek*, just a few little drops. The big news was he had done a major interview with *Playboy*.

At work, a male friend brought me the article. On Friday December fifth when leaving work I stopped for a moment with the sun shining in my face. I thought, John, we are so lucky you made it through all those years. That nobody ever took a shot at you, so many others were killed.

At the time I was doing a University Without Walls program at a private liberal school in Vermont. I was in the process of doing a thesis in creative writing for completion of my degree. The following week was going to be very busy so I could take a two-week break at Christmas. That Monday I found that I couldn't stop working even though I also felt a heaviness and exhaustion. So I would work furiously for a while and then try to lie down but I felt compelled to get to work again. By the end of the day I had done all of the week's work except for the mindless typing of my bibliography. Thank goodness.

That night, the eighth of December I made plans to see my boyfriend with whom I had been going with off and on for many years. On the way over to his home, I heard *Starting Over* on the radio but a slightly different version than usual. Lennon moaned a lot more at the end. It stood out to me. At my friend's, about twenty to eleven he suddenly told me he wanted to hold me. As he held me I found myself crying. I didn't know why. I am very grateful that I was taken care of, that tenderness was extended to me during that moment when John was being murdered. Someone was comforting me.

At a little past eleven o' clock I suddenly felt I had to go and left quickly leaving my friend confused.

When I started driving towards home, a car appeared behind me riding my bumper very closely. He could have easily passed me but instead stayed right on me. This went on for a few miles and became unnerving. Finally he passed me but didn't zoom ahead. As we approached an intersection he slowed down to stop even though the light was green. The area was well lit because of a gas station, street light and a cemetery that had a clock face made out of plants with lots of floodlights so you could see it. I had slowed down to make a left. The driver of the other car turned around and stared at me. My jaw dropped open because I was looking at John Lennon. My mind raced. I thought, maybe this is the guy I went out with that looked like John. No, this person doesn't just look like John Lennon, he feels like John Lennon. And the stare he was hitting me with was very intense. It took my breath away. Then he turned around and sped off into the night.

I made the turn and headed home. As I got out of the car I noticed that the sky was all lit up. I imagined it was the northern lights though I had never seen them this far south. It was also very warm, sixty degrees. As I walked to my door I actually said out loud: "This is a very strange night." I walked inside, fed my cat and put water on for tea.

The phone rang. It was my Dad. He said: "Do you have the TV on?" I said, "No." He said, "Are you standing up or sitting down?" I said, "Standing up." He said, "Sit down." I sat. "John Lennon has been shot four or five times. He has been rushed to a hospital where he is struggling for his life."

I don't remember what I said to my father as I hung up the phone. My first thoughts were: "Boy, John I don't know anyone who gets hit harder and more often in life then myself other then you. This is going be your hardest one yet to come through. This is going to take some time." My mind then heard again "shot four or five times" and I realized he was not going to come through this. I turned on the radio. The deejay at that moment said: "Yes, it's true. John Lennon has been killed." He began to play *Imagine*.

My mind exploded. My heart burst. I started to scream. I think it's good that I exploded rather than imploded. It was a touchy moment in my own existence. The pain was so great. I really didn't know how to live without him. I seemed to get so much strength and support from him for my perception of reality. So few people made sense to me. And he had power, incredible power. So few that saw and lived life as he did have such influence. We really needed this guy. He represented the new consciousness in such a big way. He was a huge billboard for the entire world representing a new world moving towards peace and equality for both sexes and all races. Spirituality blended with humanness combined with humor and creativity. This was a human being worth having. The loss struck to my core.

One of John's most powerful statements was the image he left us with on the cover of the *Rolling Stone* magazine's tribute issue released soon after his passing. Naked, with the clothed Yoko wrapped around him. He in all his vulnerability is showing the world his love, value and need of his woman. He is totally surrendered to the feminine. This photograph was taken hours before he died.

I can't even begin to comprehend what it was like for Yoko. No one was holding her; she was standing right beside him. I remember her line from a song written soon afterward: "I get down on my knees to throw up life." I bet you did. My world felt shattered and I never met the man. The implications for Yoko's grief were heartbreaking.

A DREAM

About two months after John died, I had a dream. It began as I was driving a car with a box of doughnuts beside me on the seat. I read in a dream book that they actually have spiritual significance! I was on my way to visit John Lennon in the hospital. Upon arrival I walked up to the nurse's station and said I was here to visit John Lennon. She said she would go and speak with him and returned shortly and said he would see me.

I was somewhat surprised and pretty excited about this and quickly went to his room where I found him wearing his striped pajamas from the famous bed-ins for peace. He told me he had gone through a pretty long recovery and asked me to help him. He said he wanted me to help him feel and release all of the fear and pain he had felt at the time of his death. At this point he asked me to lean over and he draped himself over my back. I actually felt much unprepared for this and asked him to get down.

I then went through a quick but deep internal process where I thought to myself: "how can you turn this person away, he has done so much for your life, you really need to do something for him, you can't turn him down," I had to find the courage to do this. So I said OK, I will do it, I am ready. He climbed onto my back and was dangling over me and I was supporting his full weight. He started to release all of the fear, mental anguish and physical pain he had felt when he was shot and dying. There was a lot- he lasted a long time for someone with 4 bullets in his back. He climbed the stairs into the Dakota office before collapsing onto the desk. I felt all that pain pass through my body and release through the floor. I remember nothing more except a sense of awaking exhausted and drained. I still remember this vividly and it's over 30 years ago. Anything for John.

MY LIFE'S LOSS OF JOHN LENNON 25 YEARS LATER

I actually remember that when it happened, while the pain was so acute, the world's attention so riveted on the event, that someday it would be twenty five years since it happened, a significant anniversary. How would I feel then? Would I still hurt? Would I still care for John Lennon in the same way? I would be so much older then. Would the world still remember him or would he have faded away?

I still care, the world still cares. *Imagine* is often recognized as the greatest song ever written because of its vision of humans finally grown up enough to stop fighting and share. Any new Beatles music still reaches #1 when reintroduced to yet another generation.

For me I still struggle in a world I hoped would be better by now from the efforts he and so many others have made for peace. I had thought there would be equality among races and gender and the love of life through music to have become a priority for the entire world.

As much as the political global arena may have only become worse, on a personal level, I feel his message getting stronger, person by person, as we each connect deeper to our emotions and spirituality, growing in awareness and tolerance, caring for our environment and helping others in need. Slowly the tide is turning; there is still hope "for the world to live as one."

Watching the person who took John's life on the television did leave me depressed. I saw the worst part of myself of course, interpreting one's life as a string of failures without developing an identity and latching on to John Lennon. I want to find solace in a deeper meaning to Lennon's passing in that way, that all the world-wide mourning after his death, changed us in some way, improved us, woke us up, prioritized learning the deeper meaning of life, moved us along spiritually, helped us, changed us for the better. I don't want his death to have been in vain, I hope that it was part of the plan somehow to wake us up and change us, the world. Lennon himself was such a towering standard that the music world was accountable simply by his presence on the planet. He held the energy of integrity, he stood up loud and big enough for us all to see and hear and spoke about what really mattered; that we love each other and work towards peace. No one else has the guts to say it with that much power, conviction and action. His words and deeds are passed down to generation after generation but he is sorely missed from the planet. He did his part and then split. I hope he is doing well. What of Yoko and Sean and Julian? They paid such a hard price. Yoko will be dealing with being without him for twenty-five years on a personal basis while his voice and image inundate the world she lives in.

YOKO

Yoko/Cynthia

Yoko story starts with Cynthia, John Lennon's first wife. Cynthia kept him alive so he could get to Yoko and Yoko kept him alive so he could get to us. Cynthia is a strong and good person that John was very lucky to have in his life during the early Beatle years. As much as John balked at being tied down (barely) during those wild years, if he was totally untethered he may not have made it through. I believe John needed the stability that Cynthia and their son Julian gave him during that time as much as he derided and abused it. As much as John felt his marriage and child held him back, I believe Cynthia and Julian gave him something to hold onto when his life was so out of control. With John's excesses due to his wounds and insecurities, it helped him to be anchored to a family, people who really cared about him. I don't know if he knew that then or could ever have admitted it to himself but I'm sure his soul knew.

After reading Cynthia Lennon's latest book *John* I am glad that all is finally out and said. She told her story well. I'm glad she finally stood up enough for herself to tell it. Hey, I was here too, and I exist. So does Julian. All you've heard about Yoko and John, well before that there was Cyn and John and Julian. It's a wonder she's not insane or bitterly seething mad from seeing the world view him as an icon of peace and love while he treated her with such disdain.

I had the opportunity to meet her in person and ask her after his passing: "If she could talk to John now, what would she say to him?" Cynthia said she hoped "he was finally a peace filled person." It's so interesting to see how celebrities get to play out their needs onto the global screen. In John's case, it was a circular process. I believe that John projected onto the world's arena his personal need for peace but then it's reflected back to each one of us to utilize, to find our personal peace. This ultimately would be the world's peace.

So was Lennon a phony? No, I believe his intentions and destiny were of the highest, but he was all too human. His ego may have gone so far as to be embarrassed by Cynthia and Julian and his Liverpool working class past. He wanted to become a really cool guy with a really cool woman like Yoko. Cynthia was so traditional and Yoko so cutting edge and so in tune with all that was happening in those days. He was too young and needy to get a glimpse of how cruel he was being. It's hard to understand the money though, he gave Cynthia and Julian very little to live on after their divorce. I don't know how he could have been so cheap, when he had so much money. Yoko eventually rectified this for Julian, which is wonderful. I think, had John lived, he would have come full circle, woke up to his behavior, and hopefully, rectified with Cynthia as well as Julian. It looks like he was truly getting there with Julian.

I see my own behavior reflected in John. How can I turn cold on a boyfriend or friend years ago when "something better came along." It horrifies me to think I could be so superficial, so calculating, and so selfish. But that's what we do "before love comes to town." (Bono,U2)

Lennon's life was so about growth and self-change and reflecting to the world what we all need so badly, inner and outer peace.

I somehow feel quieter inside now that Cynthia has finally let it all out. That needed to happen. We needed to know that about John and Cynthia really needed to tell it. I was always so afraid of what her truth might be. I understood about the coldness and the temper but I must say I was relieved to find out he only hit her once, I was really afraid he could have been a real constant physical abuser. So he wasn't as bad as I thought he might be!

John has been quoted as saying: "I am a violent man who has learned not to be violent and regrets his violence."

I remember in his final interview on the last day of his life he spoke about wanting to be a loving person. To have gotten there, to know that's what it is really all about, to have grown enough to want that, shows triumph. He worked with himself so hard and that's what he modeled for the rest of us. It's what we are all intimately aspiring to whether we are conscious enough at our own stage of the game to know it and that desire and that struggle was shown to us all by John Lennon.

Julian also deserves serious credit for who he has become and all he has worked through. Seeming bitter and angry for many years, and understandably so, his soul has worked past this to create the song *Beautiful* for his father. The lyrics are a deeply felt acknowledgment of his father's integrity and sacrifice for the world. Julian also mentions his personal learning from his dad about expressing emotions. Julian's postings on Facebook reveal a social consciousness, spirituality and wisdom along with an absurdist sense of humor. Remind us of anyone?

131

Yoko was Lennon's creative and intellectual equal. As beautiful and incredible as the Beatles music is, I feel Lennon's real mission was accomplished after the Beatles broke up. The Beatles set him up on the world's stage. When I was watching the Beatles in person in August of '66 one of my main thoughts was towards Lennon: "Ok, Superman, when are you going into the phone booth and changing into being who you really are and doing what you really came here to do?" That happened with Yoko. His great mission was to reveal himself to us all in all his vulnerability, insecurity and neediness so we could see that in all his greatness he shared with us those feelings, -- feelings we all try to not see in ourselves and we'd assume someone like John Lennon never has.

It's an understatement to say that Yoko lives "outside the box." Lennon waited a long time before she showed up so he could bring that side of himself out. My god, when will we as a human race wake up and realize that life on this planet could be anything we want it to be. Life isn't " the way it is", we created this but, we aren't stuck in this!!! It could be wonderful just as easily as it is to be violent and mean as it too often is now.

People laughed at John and Yoko for being naive and dumb but they were brilliant. They could step outside of the conventional mindset and IMAGINE something different. War is Over IF YOU WANT IT, like the 60's slogan, what if somebody gave a war and nobody came. If we changed inside, the whole planet could be living at higher and higher levels of creativity and kindness. It's as much a possibility as us blowing ourselves up. I'm certainly noticing that it's been over 30 years since this man passed on and as much criticism as he endured, the world is still quite fascinated by him. This proves my case: he touched a part of us that <u>does</u> know, that <u>does</u> believe, and that <u>does</u> want peace in our lives.

John and Yoko began their public relationship with a naked album cover. It was not about sexuality or profanity. It was about being willing to be literally "naked to the world" on an emotional, psychological and spiritual level. It was an act of genuine power that opened up energy channels in us all. He was willing to go to the depths of his authenticity by physically presenting himself naked to the world without any protection. He established his intimacy with us. This enabled him to communicate with us from his soul. I say John Lennon's life was about bringing oneness awareness to the planet. There are so many of us united in knowing who he is and his message of peace. He communicated with us from oneness. It was about being that vulnerable and real in order to connect with humanity.

At that depth, it opened up the channel to us all for what they would do and teach us. It was a gesture of total commitment to us, having no barriers so he could speak directly to the highest part of ourselves. It was an act of bravery and courage for someone so famous in the entertainment world to present himself without any glamour, image or facade. He shared the details of his life and hopes and dreams of his heart. His communications were always vulnerable and presented as if we knew him personally. A friend recently said she felt like she had a personal relationship with him but then said that everybody feels like that. Ah ha! The point exactly! He lived his life from oneness so we all have an intimate relationship with him. "I hope someday you'll join us and the world will live as one." I write this from the point of Lennon because it was his position in the world that made this so powerful. I totally acknowledge Yoko standing beside him, contributing and suggesting many of the main ideas, and in so many ways the teacher and fellow traveler.

John talked about posing naked for the album cover as being part of he and Yoko's getting together and how they felt like two virgins. Their love was so different and deeper than anything they ever experienced before. All that I said before was behind that feeling. They must have connected at such a pure and genuinely innocent high level of consciousness. If you consider what they created with their relationship on the global stage for us all to grow and to perhaps step outside of our trapped souls... and to consider the planet surrounded in peace and love... without war and greed....we all know and want this, it is our destiny as we grow past our ego.

It has always concerned me that the world claimed to love John Lennon so much and then was so cruel to his savior, Yoko. This just proves the illusion and worthlessness of the world's adoration. This man had it all to an absurd degree but needed so much on an emotional level. Yoko had the brains and power to give it to him. Yet the world scoffed and scorned her and does to this day. I would imagine his contempt for his fame only grew worse. We love you John but the person who finally helped you and gave you peace and safety, well, we hate her and we're going to insult her and you every chance we get. Oh yeah, the adoring masses, try and cash that in for something you really need.

I found her brilliant beyond words. On her LP, *FLY,* John plays acoustic guitar while Yoko sings: "Will you touch me, will you hold me when my mind is full of tears, and will you kiss me when my mind is so dark. All my life the doors kept closing on me and nothing in the world can open my heart but some kindness. Will you touch me when I am shaking in fear, will you reach me when I am trembling with tears?" I share these feelings with her and am grateful to her for revealing them with the intimacy and realness it reveals in their relationship. It helped me create a relationship like that for myself and my husband. Thank you so much, John and Yoko.

I admire her spiritual understanding of love in terms of being all that we need to give, along with her grasp of feminism. One of my favorites was a song on her LP, *Approximately Infinite Universe*. There was a background chorus of men, including John, singing "We are all would-be presidents of the United States." This is a result of the pressure and expectation put onto men. "This is who you need to grow up to be," or you are totally worthless.

On a deep level, John Lennon was such a "real" man to be with such a powerful, talented and enlightened woman. He was such a true friend to the return of the feminine energies in the world. But there he was stuck being "Beatle John" and the world that he moved in was clueless to these deeper artistic, intellectual and spiritual teachings. We just want to tap our feet to the music, John. We don't want to examine ourselves to find our prejudices and hypocrisies or how we are conditioned and hypnotized. We just want to get high and numb out to the great sound that you make. Let's not start to get real. I don't want you to teach me anything.

Yoko had at her fingertips total comprehension of all the latest teachings coming from the most creative artists and thinkers of our time and she taught them to John and together they were here to teach us.

THE FEMINIZATION OF SOCIETY

BY YOKO ONO, FEBRUARY 1972

In the summer of 1972 Yoko Ono wrote a piece called The Feminization of Society for the New York Times. This is a feeling and insightful piece revealing her depth and dedication. I can only quote from the writing here but it is well worth finding its entirety on the Internet.

Yoko shares with us her concerns that "If we try to achieve our freedom within the framework of the existing social set-up, men, will continue to make a token gesture of giving us a place in their world. Some of us will succeed in moving into elitist jobs, kicking our sisters on the way up...or being conned into thinking that joining the male perversions and madness is what equality is all about: 'join the army'...etc."

"The ultimate goal of female liberation is not just to escape from male oppression. How about liberating ourselves from our various mind trips such as ignorance, greed, masochism, fear of God and social conventions?"

"We must make more positive usage of the feminine tendencies of the society which, up to now, have been either suppressed or dismissed as something harmful, impractical, irrelevant and ultimately shameful."

"I am proposing a feminization of society; the use of feminine nature as a positive force to change the world. We can change ourselves with feminine intelligence and awareness, into a basically organic, noncompetitive society based on love, rather than reasoning. The result will be a society of balance, peace and contentment. We can evolve rather than revolt, come together rather than claim independence, and feel rather than think. These are characteristics that are considered feminine; characteristics that men despise in women. But have men really done so well by avoiding the development of these characteristics within themselves?"

My thoughts:

Nothing is inherent in value. We are giving everything its value. Lip service has always been paid to the value of raising children and making a home but we can see the fallacy in our fragile, dysfunctional society.

I remember as a child making a list of the same job performed by women and men and the value and prestige attached to when the male did it. One example was women making dinner every night for her family with barely a thank you. If the male (in those days) chef was making dinner in a restaurant, he would have accolades, status and big money.

We still have not changed the basic paradigm about what has value. Male values of running a company are still seen as the highest prestigious positions and too often with the old attributes of ruthless competition and exploitation of people, animals and the earth. Yes, women can be a "success" but we must leave behind our feminine qualities of nurturing and caring and become as hard and cold as men in the traditional business world. Yes, we made it but we became as a man to get it. That's not the change we needed.

It is not a gender issue. It is a masculine/feminine qualities issue. I remember reading where a feminist was upset because she saw women taking positions in the world but mostly in the service professions; doctors, social workers and psychologists. She considered this a failure. This was because the qualities of care taking were still being devalued and dismissed. How can we build a kinder world when these feminine attributes are still being rejected and seen as worthless? We desperately need to take care of each other physically and emotionally.

It is hard to say because of the lip service paid but what could possibly be more important than raising children and teaching them to love and respect themselves as well as everyone else, animals and the earth? Cooking healthy food and a home of sanctuary and encouragement is creating the future for all of humanity. There is nothing wrong with this profession other then it not being valued in any genuine capacity. By definition that it was traditionally done by a woman and not a man made it worthless. It in itself is the greatest contribution anyone can make. The freedom to choose is so important, so many still have children because "it's what you do." If only those who truly wanted children had them, we would automatically be better off by less population exasperating our global problems. Children brought up wanted and truly cared for would lessen our violence and lack of caring for each other and the earth.

A woman can also choose to make her way in the world that is creative and contributes in a positive way to society or any combination of the two. I've lived like that, it is just how it is done that matters so much. The value needs to be inherent in whatever a woman does, not that what she is doing gives her value.

I've always felt that the masculine qualities of action and power would be much better if tempered within the feminine qualities of gentleness and nurturing. Masculine qualities left rogue lead to violence and conquest over others. This energy placed within the qualities of caretaking and cooperation provides us with the energy and focus to bring about needed changes in our society and world. I noticed some time ago how the nouns like woman/man and the pronouns like he/she/her are used in our language. We grew up only using the masculine words when referring to humanity or as pronouns in writing. The masculine versions of the words exclude the feminine. The female versions include the masculine. Man is in Woman. He is within the words "she and her." All along we could have been using the feminine versions and all would have been represented. Even now, writers who strive to be politically correct use both. Again we are still within the male paradigm – just using the feminine version would be simpler.

The question needs to be: when we, men and women, are in the world, how are we doing it?

Are we approaching business interactions with kindness, gentleness, cooperation and love or with ruthless, calculating, manipulative competition? Are we recognizing the other as oneself ("I am he as you are me and we are all together") or someone we use to get to the supposed next level of society? "First we must learn how to smile as we kill if we want to be like the folks on the hill" *Working Class Hero* by John Lennon

Veganism

One of the greatest movements that has come out of the new compassionate awareness that began in the 60's is vegetarianism and now evolving into veganism and the raw food movement.

I believe that meat is more of a drug than nourishment. It keeps us grounded to the earth and dulls our awareness of the higher realms of spirit as well as keeping us from feeling our emotional pain.

For me I choose not to eat meat for many reasons but my biggest argument is with the factory farms. Please educate yourself to the depth of suffering that animals are experiencing and consider eating something else. Please don't believe anyone who tells you that you need to eat meat for your health. Consider that the truth is really quite the opposite. Especially with all the drugs used to keep the animals alive in their filthy cramped conditions. If nothing else, consider that when you consume these animals you are ingesting all of this suffering and the fear experienced at the time of their death. We all know about the chemicals released into the body when under stress. You're eating this! The effects of raising cows is destroying our rain forests thus our air quality and environment. As Paul McCartney has said "the biggest thing you can do for the earth is stop eating meat." Paul has also said: "If slaughterhouses had glass walls, everyone would be vegetarian."

Vegans have moved on to releasing the need for dairy cows which also inflicts cruelty, stealing babies from their mothers and raising them to become veal. These babies live in crates where they cannot move and are covered in their excrement. Bon appetite! Dairy products also cause much discomfort in our bodies given all the hormones, antibiotics and other chemicals added to their diets which all pass through to our human systems. The effects on our young girls is evident - girls are developing much younger in terms of starting their periods as well as in their breast development.

The Raw movement seems to have taken this is to its brilliant and natural conclusion. Non-processed organic food is the most full of life energy with nothing that is detrimental to the body. So much of what we have been taught to eat is actually wearing out the body and is causing many diseases.

The process involved in going from a classic meat filled diet to one of mostly fruits, nuts, seeds and vegetables is a journey and needs to be taken with time and awareness. The best way to start is to concentrate on choosing and adding in fresh organic foods. When the 4:00 slump hits, reach for fruit rather than sugar. Have salads as often as you can enjoy. Let the less healthy food start to slip away rather than doing anything that sets up a feeling of denial or restraint. These feelings tend to avenge themselves.

I really connected with Paul and Linda on this issue. There is a story Linda told of cooking a lamb leg in the pot and looking out the window at their beautiful sheep and lambs and making the connection from her heart to her head. They became two of the world's largest profile proponents of vegetarianism and animal rights. I love the recipes in Linda's cookbook as they are wonderful transitional meals from meat to non-meat. They also got very involved with animal rights organizations like PETA and Friends of the Earth. I went to a McCartney concert where he actually got the stadium to sell only veggie hot dogs. The guy in back of me discovered how delicious they were. I am often shocked that someone cringes when I eat a tofu hot dog when they are eating a regular one consisting of eyeballs, intestines and killing floor scrapings.

People often speak to me of their food sensitivities to gluten, grains, soy and sugar for good reason. I respect their concerns for what these foods are doing to their body. And I wonder what the mutilation, torture, rape, confinement and murder of conscious, intelligent animals is doing to their soul. Friends sometimes gleefully eat their meat and even wave their meat at me when we share a meal. I often want to ask if you were dining with Paul McCartney, would you be eating that.

Having dedicated my life to making earth a more peaceful planet, letting go of the violence and cruelty of eating meat, fish and dairy is one action that I can take.

Inspiration from Ringo

I really admire how Ringo really recreated himself from the depths of addiction. Not an easy fate being a decidedly #4 Beatle. There are jokes about the Beatles being 3 immensely talented people and one extraordinarily lucky bastard. I also believe he could possibly have feelings of guilt concerning Pete Best and whatever childhood pain he carries from his father leaving and his illness.

I read where Ringo was drinking 16 bottles of wine a day. I still try to fathom if this is possible. But perhaps, given the lifestyle that started back in Liverpool in the 60's and the 70's, it was understandable to accept the indulgences of the rich and famous.

Ringo cleaned himself up and teamed up with other talented musicians of that time and has enjoyed many years performing and traveling the world with his shows. He seemed to have come to accept himself as he is and utilize the talents while bolstering the talents of others. Ringo gifted them with opportunities of stardom while performing after their shooting stars had fallen.

I remember reading that he says he lives on vegetables, fruit and water. Think of that. I do believe that is correct. It is my goal as well. I look at him; he's so slim and light on his feet and has so much energy. His story is one of triumph, self-acceptance, and joy. Behold the Ringo.

For Paul: *Eleanor Rigby*

The feeling of sadness and loneliness in this song about Eleanor Rigby matched the feelings emanating from my mother. I would often shed a tear when I listened tuning into my mother's emotional pain. She spent day after day alone, unwanted and believing she was unloved. I was glad when she died that it wasn't quite as bad as it was for Eleanor, family and my friends were there. I spoke the eulogy honoring her as best I could.

For George: *Within You Without You*

When we speak of Oneness, George refers to the ego as the "space between us all" and the "love we all could share once we find it." The words are so bold and powerful and most significant for me. "Try to realize it's all within yourself, no one else can make you change." That the only way we really change is through deep self-awareness, through meditation as we develop the perspective of our witness self, the part of us that sit behind our behavior and observes and through deep examination, change it for the better.

This was a big turning point for me, understanding that the work I needed to do was about me, being an internal examination and process of transformation that I needed to undertake. This has become my focus in life -, working through the layers of defenses and projections of my personality in order to find the connection I feel for all people and creatures of the earth.

For George: *While My Guitar Gently Weeps*

Along with *Imagine* and *Morning Has Broken* by Cat Stevens, I'd like to include *While My Guitar Gently Weeps* as the songs I want played at my wake.

For me the lyrics of this song express the deep ache in me from believing we can be living in a kind world based on love. He begins with the line "I look at you all see the love there that's sleeping" Oh I believe this to be so. A favorite quote of mine along the same lines is "In everyone there sleeps a sense of life lived according to love." Philip Larkin

George goes on to say that "no one has told us how to unfold our love." For me my religious upbringing did not, it was about how bad I was and how much of a sinner, not how to feel love for myself or others or how to live my life from a place of kindness and sharing. Jesus spoke of this in the Bible but that is not what the Christian church was instructing me on. For me John describes what this world would be like in *Imagine*. And for me if we can imagine it, it must be possible or we wouldn't be able to think of it.

George talks about us being "controlled, diverted and perverted". "No one has alerted" us to how the ego, the belief in our separateness has tricked us into manipulating and using each other. We can never win this game because we are only hurting ourselves.

Isn't It a Pity

When I found out in the early morning of George's passing, this is the song I first put on and cried as I swayed to the music. Again George so beautifully shares the tragedy of most human relationships and our unawares of the spiritual world: "as we take each other's love without thinking anymore, forgetting to give back, isn't it a pity." And because of all the tears, their eyes can't hope to see, the beauty that surrounds them, isn't it a pity, how we break each other's hearts and cause each other pain." We too often take each other for granted and let misunderstandings build up until a relationship is lost. And with all our pain we cannot see how beautiful life can be.

BEATLE FRIENDS AND FAMILY

BEATLE FRIENDS

Throughout my life I have had friends who have shared my love of the Beatles. There had been three up until 2003 and then I hit the mother lode and found what feels like my Beatle family.

My first Beatle friend I had from the start of the Beatles on Ed Sullivan but it was a bit on the dark side. Originally, her favorite Beatle was Ringo and mine was of course, John. We started to argue over who was the better Beatle. I felt like, especially with Ringo that she was egging me on, I didn't really have anything against Ringo but I certainly was going to defend John. We would actually be standing there screaming at each other about whose Beatle was best.

Then the stakes got a lot higher when Ringo got married so she felt Ringo could no longer be her favorite Beatle and chose Paul. Now, she truly had an opponent. I felt strongly so we really got at it. We would be in each other's faces insulting each other's Beatle, yelling as loud as we could. This then escalated into tearing up pictures of Paul and John. When she would go home the floor of my room would be covered with ripped up magazines. I often felt great regret; all my favorite pictures got ripped up. Luckily, most of the magazines were replaceable and I eventually would buy two copies of them so I could hide one copy.

It's interesting to think what we were playing out there. Certainly neither of us was having happy childhoods so a lot of our anger and frustration got displaced by carrying on like this. So I would say it did us well but it's strange to think back on it.

I remember at one point she called me and told me she named her pillows Ringo and John. She was sleeping with Ringo and threw John on the floor. So I named my pillows Ringo and John. I laid my head on Ringo and hugged John. I even wrote their names in permanent marker on the inside of the pillow so I would know who was who. Till this day I still need to hug a pillow to sleep.

My other childhood Beatle friend and I met in homeroom in 7th grade. Her home life held a fascination to me because it was totally different than my own and my other friends. When I would visit I would hear her family having animated, lively, happy discussions going on in the kitchen. Everyone greeted me with a smile, I felt welcome. I asked my friend if her parents ever fought and she told me once they did and her mother went and sat in a shopping parking lot for two hours and then returned home. It was wonderful to see an environment like this did exist and I really enjoyed my time with my friend in her room calmly enjoying our love of the Beatles. When she graduated from high school her grandmother treated her to a trip through Europe and I was gifted with a cup from King's road in London. Forty years later it still sat beside me holding my pens at the computer when she and I found each other again through a class reunion. With anticipation we asked each other the big question: "Do you still love the Beatles?" A big yes from both us brought us together to begin enjoying each other and Beatle events all over again.

In a recent conversation: She said: "Everybody close to me in my life associates me with liking the Beatles. Yet, when I started going on Beatle tours in England, flying all over to go to Beatle conventions, and Paul McCartney concerts, I could tell that people thought I was being obsessive and trying to live in the past (like it was somehow emotionally unhealthy). I felt that I had to justify my long-standing interest in the Beatles. Just because I'm older and more mature, I should have outgrown my fascination with the Beatles. Yet nobody raises an eyebrow if someone likes to collect stamps, or dolls, or model airplanes their whole life!"

I responded: "Yes, isn't that something, it's funny, my big change was actually after 911. I thought to myself, "I spend my free time enjoying the Beatles, not taking air pilot lessons to fly a plane into a building. I am a harmless human being. I will never let anyone make me feel bad about myself or ever apologize for loving the Beatles ever again!"

The closest friendship I ever experienced began through the Beatles while living at the spiritual community. I had been there a little over a month and in a new person's orientation meeting. She was sitting across from me. It was a big room and she was very far away, so we couldn't really get a close look at each other nor have eye contact. But her name was the same as mine and it is was an unusual name. It was a name that had haunted me all my life because it was odd. Like me. So, wow, there's another one. She really stood out to me. I don't think it was just the name. I felt we already knew each other well.

A few days later I was chatting with one of the guys living there and I heard myself spontaneously say: "John Lennon was my first guru." He responded: "Someone else told me John Lennon was their first guru. The other woman with your name, that's who."

I also had the phrase John Lennon had blond hair floating through my head. When I saw the Beatles I was surprised to see that John's hair was blond. Who knew? I thought he must have been one of those people whose hair turns blond in the summer sun. Doesn't really show up in the photos, never read it mentioned.

I don't actually remember how she and I approached each other but I do know that we made plans to meet in the lounge one evening and share a pint of Rice Dream and talk John Lennon.

She quickly told me she saw John outside the Dakota once, the summer of 1980. She didn't think it was him at first because his hair was blond but her knees were knocking together so hard, she knew it had to be him. We also soon realized we had both been published in the booklet The Fest for Beatle Fans put out after John died. We had both noticed the other person with our name. Now here we both were living in the same spiritual community.

And so began the closest female friendship of my life. A friendship in its height that brought me the opportunities to share more of myself up to then I ever had with another person. For the first time I had someone who shared my point of view, my values, my beliefs and loved Beatle music and could really experience joy and enthusiasm. We became roommates and began to get to know each other. We discovered we both had pain filled childhoods. We both had mothers that were sick when we grew up. Mine went crazy, hers died. Not all that long ago. Mine would die soon. She was the only person of my later friends who would meet her.

We had so much fun together! When we saw each other in the

halls we would trade banter from Beatle movies, she would stomp her foot like John did in concerts. Having someone to share my Beatle love in such detail brought me so much joy. She had a walk- man type tape player that had two entries for headphones. Before we had to report for seva (work) we would put our earphones on together and dance in place smiling at each other listening to a Beatle song. In March we ventured to the Fest for Beatle Fans together, finally having someone to share it all with that felt the same level of enthusiasm. I remember she even got me up to dance during the concert, my favorite thing to do! Our best laugh was that after our long drive back to the community, when we entered the drive way, people were already up jogging. Oh dear. We were really tired at seva that day, but shared a really satisfying secret. She really lifted my spirits. I finally wasn't so alone in my life.

We also shared a great love of animals. Cats had always been my other love, birds for her. We both were vegetarians, very aware of the suffering of animals, the effects of eating meat on the environment, etc. We could talk for hours about these subjects, including political discussions and at times comforting each other about our childhood pain.

She left the community in a year but continued to visit. We still had so much fun. She brought me lots of tapes of current music. We lived on a limited stipend in the community and my friend would generously treat me to meals out and a new piece of clothing. Then we discovered U2. Here's a live one. Bono, a living Lennon, another rock star that stood for social change and deep truth. Oh boy!! She brought me music and videos of U2. We went to see U2 at Madison Square were we shared a special moment. We were in the last row on the floor. When

Bono walked on stage I felt every one of his footfalls and the organ of *Streets with No Name* slowly getting louder, the sunrise like light brightening behind him. Bono wore a cowboy hat with his hair pulled back. Part way through the first song while I was looking through the binoculars, off came the hat and the leather strip holding back his hair. "His hair is loose", I mused. In a split second my neck was being whipped around as my friend grabbed the binoculars from me with their string still around my neck. We laughed about it over and over for years. We just had to look at each other and repeat "His hair is loose." We'd laugh and pass that knowing look.

My Beatle Family

One year and one week after my father passed on my life began anew. On March 9th 2003 Andre Gardner's Breakfast with the Beatles hit the road! Andre, radio personality extraordinaire, refers to himself as a card carrying bald Beatle freak! Andre started to broadcast his show live on Sunday morning from area restaurants every couple of months for several years. Andre in my opinion offers the best Beatle show available because of his passion, expertise and the effort he puts into the show with rarities, interviews, covers, alternate mixes, rock band isolations and overall enthusiasm.

The first show broadcast from a restaurant was really special. The staff wore Beatle wigs and offered the finest all you can drink Bloody Mary bar, we still talk about it to this day and smile. Mr. Puppet was there with his fabulous John Lennon in his long hair and white suit puppet and Andre was spinning the Beatle hits. The place was packed with local Beatle fans who had been listening to the show but now got to meet each other and interact. As our family grew we eventually found out that quite a few of us were there that day but had not met. We wished we could go back in time and experience the show and the Bloody Marys together.

I did meet Judy, Beatle sister number one that day. The restaurant was in a strip mall and as my husband and I drove through the parking lot this gorgeous tall slim woman dressed in black with fabulous cowboy boots came strutting down the slight hill. God could not have made her any easier to notice and when we were seated, there she was right next to me on the long banquette. She was not with anyone. She later explained her friend had needed to cancel at the last minute. I do feel this was serendipitous because I might not have reached out to her if she was not alone. But say hello and introduce ourselves we did and we hit it off and best of all she asked me to dance before long and we were the first ones up which would set a precedent for our Beatle sisterhood as time went on.

The next breakfast was downtown and my husband and I planned to meet Judy there and sit together. It was cold and rainy and we had to stand outside and wait to get in but the food was great and again had a lot of fun. At the end of the show Andre held a trivia contest that a pretty blond woman won. After Rob and I left Judy began a conversation with her and Susan became our next Beatle sister. I was lucky enough to meet her in the summer when Andre had the first BWTB cruise aboard a ship sailing down a river.

The next person I remember was a guy who just kept appearing in our presence. He was at all the road shows and always seemed to be seated near us, or at our large banquet style table. When I went to other local events or concerts revolving around the Beatles, I always saw him standing there....I even noticed that he and his girlfriend were in the room next to ours at The Fest for Beatle Fans at a hotel with 14 floors! At what turned out to be the last restaurant broadcast beside the boat trips for quite a while, he approached our table where my husband, Judy, Susan and I were seated and asked if we wanted to be put on his Beatle email list. We all said yes and now we had finally met our Beatle brother, Geno.

Geno is involved with the Lehigh Valley Music Awards, an organization that honors, promotes and rewards musicians that perform consistently in the valley. Each year Geno contributes to creating a Beatle themed performance.

At next Fest as my husband and I descended the staircase from the second floor where Geno introduced us to his girlfriend Marianne. She and I quickly discovered we had both been attending the Fest since the very first one in 1974. I knew I had met my Beatle twin sister. Marianne commented once that all of our friends love the Beatles but she and I "live like it's 1964." I love this sentiment. I always saw Geno and Marianne as the king and queen of the Beatle prom. My own heart broke when they parted a few years later. Through Geno and Marianne we met young Ryan, Beatle fan and expert born several months before John Lennon's passing. Ryan had one of the best and unusual memorabilia collections I have ever seen. He joined us for many events and parties for a few years till he jilted the Beatles for Pink Floyd.

Geno also introduced us to wonderful Maureen who was Sid Bernstein's publicist. Sid is well known for bringing the Beatles to Carnegie Hall in 1964 and beginning the stadium rock shows by booking the Beatles into Shea in 65 and 66. He also promoted many of the British invasion groups of the 60's.

Maureen's life took a big step forward in happiness when she met Franco who is gloriously friendly and quickly involved himself in all of our activities and created many others for us. Maureen and Franco are now married and held their ceremony at Strawberry Fields in Central Park in NYC. Friends, family and lucky bystanders surrounded them at the Imagine Mosaic as they said their vows. Susana Bastarrica led the ceremony. Susana works at the United Nations and creates many peace vigils throughout New York City. During the wedding, a man waved a beautiful large flag with a white dove of peace and a string quartet played Strawberry Fields Forever. The Imagine Mosaic is a power place for peace and I feel this ceremony added to its power.

I also met Janice, a fellow John Lennon fan, and her two lovely daughters. Watching them enjoy each other and the Beatles together was very healing. Gary, a retired NYC fireman who Marianne met on line outside a Paul McCartney concert joined us with his girlfriend Carol, a wonderful outgoing person.

In June of 2006 Paul McCartney was actually going to turn the much sung- about age of 64. When he originally sang *When I'm 64* he was in his twenties and we were in our teens. The thought of this was laughable but here it was. I felt this had to be commemorated and created what turned out to be the first of many Beatle parties. We had a Beatle sing along with some of my husband's band mates, learned that Susan was an extraordinary singer, watched the Beatles do Shakespeare and laughed and shared some great local pizza. Big fun began.

Worth noting that at the same Beatle breakfast that we met Geno, Susan told us she had just learned about a local Beatle band called Almost Fab that played at a beautiful old inn. She said we should go. We went the next month and began another dimension to the Beatle fun we shared together. Turned out Almost Fab was far from an average bar band and as good as the best of the professionals, as they put on a great show. And the Inn was not any dive bar but a beautiful old Victorian with a formal dining room with a great chef. The band played in a nice room decorated wonderfully and on our first visit, quite festive for the holidays. Over the years Toni and Mark who owned the inn turned out to be really warm and friendly. They always welcomed us when we came with our original foursome and at times up to fifteen as the word spread through our crowd about the great band we could dance to! And dance we did, Rich, our own John Lennon, always told us he loved it when we came to see them because we always got up to dance right away and that started others to dare to leave their seats and move their bodies. The hilarious part was that the band was not up on a stage, we were standing on the same floor level and we were dancing right in front of them. Our crowd was made of uninhibited dancers so our legs are flying and our arms were flailing! The dance floor was incredibly tiny so we had to stay very aware as we danced but even so, there were still a few times when we caught each other as we were about to fall into a band member as he played his guitar and sang. All the more fun!

Soon after the Cirque du Soleil Beatles LOVE show opened in Vegas our friend Geno began organizing a group trip. A list was sent around with those interested and I noticed someone named Mike who lived very nearby. I introduced myself and we began to compare histories and mutual friends that has never seemed to have stopped after many years. It's like we were in the same room for 30 years but never met each other.

We had similar parents growing up as well so I felt I had found my second Beatle brother. We met each other soon after at an Andre Gardner advance showing of *John Lennon vs. the United States of America*.

The trip to Vegas meant so much to me and was a blast from start to finish. For someone who had once loved the Beatles in solitary to have 13 people fly across the country to be together to experience this great show was happiness of the highest degree for me. Mike and his then wife Jen and my husband and I even slipped away and had a nice hike in the red rocks which are so beautiful just outside of town. Geno managed to rent us a last minute highly discounted limo for the ride to the show which made the night even more special. We were all in our glory posing for pictures in the psychedelic Revolution lounge before the show. The show was heaven as it unfolded before our eyes - complete with the Beatles speaking from outtakes during the creation of the songs. The effort put into the sets and costumes and the skill of the performers created a terrific experience. During *Within You Without You* we were all covered by a sheer white cloth, the wall of illusion perhaps. Many years later this memory still glows as a fulfilling highlight of Beatle love, friendship and joy.

Meanwhile my husband had joined a Beatle website called Beat Gear Cavern and had connected with someone who referred to herself as "60's girl." This had a charge for me immediately; I loved her name. Rob also started to mention someone that loved cats and had two like us and also liked to travel to the Lake District in England and even to the same somewhat obscure section, Lake Buttermere. The lake was deeply ensconced through winding mountain passes in the northwest. It took me awhile to understand that this was all the same person! My god! I've got to meet her and luckily learned that Joyce would be coming to the next Fest for Beatle Fans. I still remember the Friday night dance party and as the bodies parted and there she was. Sometimes when two people meet it's like a reunion and that's how it felt with Joyce. Ahhh, it's you again, great! Let's begin our dance anew. And we did eventually enjoy among many other moments a wonderful trip to Lake Buttermere staying in an apartment at the beautiful Bridge Hotel. Joyce and her husband Joe took us to our first Beatle Week in Liverpool. Beatle bands from all over the world take over the town at the end of August, which again was a Beatle lover's dream come true. I would always remember how it would be with each nationality that I encountered – the faces reflected the individual Beatles. This really was a hoot to me, a Japanese John Lennon, a Hungarian John Lennon, and a South American John Lennon and on it went. I loved this along with the fabulous music and getting to experience the bands in the venues the Beatles had played. And people who loved the Beatles filled the town.

Joyce introduced me to Terri and Pat, Michelle and Clo and Chris among others. More fun Beatle people.

Eventually Shirley, a friend who I worked with, and I began to form a close bond. She liked the Beatles but was not the expert like my Beatle family. Thus started her tutorial including a subtle finger messaging system when we hear Beatle songs she has learned who was singing and who wrote the song. She gradually saw all the movies and learned the history. This has been fun for both of us. Shirley and I also love to travel to the UK together and on our first trip met Sarah who is a life loving and celebrating soul who we connected with because of her love of cats. Eventually we found out she loves the Beatles too! So she has joined us several years now at our Beatles convention bringing much enthusiasm with her 60's outfits, decorations and especially her dress up glasses, from guitars to peace signs.

My dear friend from junior high school Cindy has now joined us which is so special for me. My husband brought us Nancy through his work - a high-spirited soul who has endeared herself to everyone.

After the first *When I'm Sixty Four* get-togethers, the Beatle Parties really got rolling. The following year was the 40th anniversary of the release of *Sgt. Peppers* so that certainly was a reason to celebrate! We turned our home into a hippie pad complete with Indian bedspread over the sofa, Champa incense, and day glo posters with black light. Mike brought us his lava lamp and we put a beautiful bamboo room divider with a psychedelic butterfly between the living and dining room. We all dressed for the part and brought pictures of ourselves to share from back in the day.

These parties included lots of Beatle decorations, trivia contests, sing-a-longs and Beatle themed cakes!

Later that year we celebrated *Magical Mystery* tour. I had bought the *Magical Mystery Tour* bus cookie jar as decoration but it had a dual purpose. . I had been at a funeral recently and the person had been cremated and was in a beautiful urn. I quickly realized that I needed something appropriate for myself when the time comes and thought a Beatle cookie jar, in particular the MMT bus (George's line "you never know when the bus is gonna come and take you away".) and of course, death is from our perspective the ultimate *Magical Mystery Tour.*

The next year we started at Ryan's to commemorate the first Ed Sullivan show and in May at Marianne's we had a Bed In Party in which we dressed in pajamas and made posters for the walls. Marianne created a cake that was in the shape of a bed and was delicious! This was after Marianne gave us the full Scarsdale tour of where Linda McCartney grew up, where Linda and Yoko went to school and the NYC tour of the Warwick and the CBS venue where the Beatles played on Ed. We also visited where Ed Sullivan is interred with our friend Benjy who is a comedian and impressionist standing in front of Ed's drawer in the mausoleum doing a very good imitation of the man. This was a hilariously absurd moment for me. This is also where John Lennon was cremated which was poignant and sad for me.

Our *Yellow Submarine* party was great fun decorated with a long poster on the front door, Yellow Sub blanket, posters, Mike's yellow sub action figures and Marianne's Yellow Submarine champagne glasses. I love champagne; this made it taste even better. I believe this is the party that Mike started making us CD's of the pop hits of the year of the party. I have this wonderful memory of a living room full of people singing with great gusto and joy *"Those Were the Days"* by McCartney's protégé Mary Hopkins. This was such a special moment to me to share the love of this music with like-minded people. And since we live in the house I grew up in we filled this once sad home with laughter and happiness. My inner child was finally getting hers.

The next party really thrilled my child self. We celebrated 45 years of Beatle music in America on February 7th, the anniversary of their arrival in 1964. This time I got to bring out my trunk of Beatle magazines from the day which I had kept because of my mother's suggestion that I would treasure having them when I was older. I really got a kick out of looking around the room and seeing people looking though issues of *16 Magazine* and *Datebook* including the fateful issue with the "We are bigger then Jesus interview" with John Lennon. I also found my original 45's which were in two record holders. Soon after my parents had gifted me with these record boxes my mother left my father and we were staying with my aunt and uncle. I had written The Beatles on the outside of the holder and one of my cousins added in big black marker STINK!! This had pained me all these years but now after a friend's suggestion I crossed out the offending word and wrote ARE GREAT!! The little moments that showed me how disempowered I had been. The thought that I could change that never occurred to me.

I had lots of fun digging around in old boxes downstairs finding what I hadn't sadly sold off of my memorabilia. I found my Beatle sneakers which fit Judy perfectly and matched her outfit as I recall. She was wearing a black and white t-shirt with Paul's grandfather from *A Hard Days Night* on the front. Found my Beatle dolls of course and my birthday card from the Beatles my parents had given me when I turned 12. I still remember opening this card with their picture on the front and inside signed with their printed autographs. This was magic to me, I was thrilled. My parents had also added the signature of my fabulous cats, a purrfect addition.

I remember this party being especially riotous for me because the Beatles *Monopoly* game had just been released so we set it up on the dining room table. Now sometime in the late 70's

I had bought a soft visor that said The Beatles across it at the Fest. As we were beginning the game, Jen exclaimed that she wanted to be banker. My mind quickly thought of the hat and with all the times I had moved and actually never worn this thing. It was hanging in the living room closet and I had it in my hands in seconds. Its big moment and purpose had finally come and it was ready. Jen looked so adorable in this visor being the banker and every time I looked at her I smiled inside at how it was just all finally coming together! I remember that Judy had been gifted with a fine bottle of champagne that she did not care for that she brought for the party. Shirley and I were sipping it happily as we played. I remember the jokes and the laughter as we played the game. I had also found my Beatles *Flip Your Wig* game and people had played that earlier set up on the coffee table. I had always used the John piece from it, when playing regular *Monopoly* over the years.

We moved the next party downtown to Joyce & Joe's. This was the Beatles in India party! The women dressed in saris we had ordered and had sent directly from India which added to the fun. We had bindis on our third eye and plenty of bangles around our arms and ankles. The guys dressed in Nehru shirts and Judy's friend Joe came dressed in a beautiful silk Indian shirt and pants. Joyce had beautiful decorations of flowers and mini union jacks to represent the English connection to the country. She had it catered with delicious Indian food completing the experience.

Our next party was Abbey Road and I told everyone to come dressed like one of the Beatles on the iconic record cover. That afternoon after praying for weeks that it would not rain, my husband and I constructed a zebra stripe on the driveway and hung a metal Abbey Road sign on the garage. I still remember Marianne's screams of joy when she pulled up and jumped out of her car to join us!! In various configurations we all posed in position on our zebra crossing and took pictures. Marianne baked the cake and had decorated it with the zebra crossing. Amazingly, shortly before, we had all been together in New York City and had found a vinyl copy of Abbey Road. We cut out the Beatles from the cover and put them on top of the cake along with a Volkswagen and the other necessary accouterments to make it perfect. This was a crowning masterpiece for Marianne.

We next celebrated the movie *Help!* This time I was able to use the posters I had made of the four doors of the house the Beatles shared in the scene in the beginning of the movie. Green, blue, white and red paper with stained glass, it was wonderful for me to rediscover the arts and crafts part of me and I was very pleased with how they turned out. Terri and Pat had a big actual movie promo cardboard cutout they had from a theater to add to the effect!

We then celebrated our ten year anniversary of the first live Beatle brunch. We of course had a brunch party even though it was Saturday night. And yes, thanks to Mike we had ourselves a wonderful Bloody Mary Bar.

The year 2014 celebrated 50 years of Beatle music in America. Our Beatles convention returned to the hotel of the first fest and on the exact weekend the Beatles first arrived in New York and appeared on Ed Sullivan. The exceptional house band Liverpool gave a great show as well as many special guests including Mark Hudson, Billy J Kramer, Chad and Jeremy and Donovan. Also for the first time was Prudence Farrow, the inspiration for my favorite Beatle song, Dear Prudence. Both Donovan and she brought the spiritual dimension to the festivities. Prudence has a deep and authentic understanding of the higher spiritual transformation happening on earth right now and is very articulate and is able to explain and communicate what is happening clearly and simply. She told us the Beatles were aware of their leadership position in this and took responsibility to bring a message of hope and love to their fans.

The next weekend was the anniversary of when the Beatles appeared on the Ed Sullivan Show in Miami. Mark Johnson and his best of the best Tribute Band 1964 played at the same hotel, the Deauville in Florida. The show was in the same room and the backdrop was re-created. Eight of us from our Beatle family went down and we were joined by one of my dear friends from the spiritual community, Sara Beth. She brought along her 12 year old son Eddie who loves Ringo as he is an aspiring drummer and has started a Beatle fan club in school. The show was fantastic, poignant and we dressed to the nines and danced with joy. A banquet followed the show with the band in attendance and the next day turned out to be a glorious beach day in the middle of a long cold snowy winter. My husband and I and our friend Shirley almost did not make it because of a flight cancellation from what seemed like endless snow storms. I stayed on the phone from 9:30 at night to 12:30 am to rebook our flight. The closest flight to Miami we could get meant we had to hire a car for a 2 ½ hour drive. We blew into town just in time to dress for the show. I was not going to miss this moment. It was all worth it. Thank you Mark Johnson and 1964.

On February 7, 2015 our Beatle family gathered to have a movie party to celebrate the 51st anniversary of Beatle music in America. We also launched the next 50 years of Beatle music in America!

Together we enjoyed watching *I Wanna Hold Your Hand*, produced by Stephen Spielberg. This is an over the top farce but yet gloriously captures the moment of the Beatles arrival and the first Ed Sullivan show. It's done with knowing detail and the slapstick had us all laughing out loud. We then watched the best documentary of the time, the Maysles Brothers *The Beatles First US Visit*. This followed the Beatles while they were here with wonderful candid moments. The train ride from New York to Washington was especially amusing. We finished off the evening with *Backbeat* which represents the time the Beatles spent in Hamburg, Germany before they hit the big time.

Beatle parties and events for me were definitely part of the "it's never too late to have a happy childhood" philosophy for me. They satisfied and healed a part of me that had been shamed and loved in solitude for too long. I am forever thankful for my life affirming, life loving Beatle family.

And you dear reader are an extension of that family, thank you.

ODE TO FEST FOR BEATLE FANS

The first Fest for Beatle Fans was held in September of 1974 with the blessing of John Lennon at the Commodore Hotel in Manhattan. We are still going strong 41 years later. I was 21 years old when I walked through the doors and felt like I had gone to Beatle Heaven. Everywhere I turned, everywhere I looked was The Beatles. I had found my world. I floated on air the entire weekend. I remember they were auctioning for charity a beautiful white guitar of John Lennon's. I was thrilled to stand before such an icon and just take it in. I heard my first live Beatle tribute band, which caught on, one could say! I saw *Magical Mystery Tour* for the first time, being mesmerized as they gently danced down the stairs in their white tuxedos. Thus began my yearly pilgrimage which has given me so many good times, made me so many friends and if only I could get across how much joy!!! The music made by so many people over the years, the stars, the professionals, the amateurs, the fans, and once even myself and two friends. There is such jubilance, the faces of bliss, the bodies dancing and moving, singing from the heart and soul. Our eyes wide open taking each other in, connecting with each other in this sea of love that Beatle music creates. What we have all shared with each other for all these years has been one of the greatest blessings of my Beatle loving life.

The first years of the Fest were still the peak of the Beatle's solo careers and even though we were a bit older, the enthusiasm for one's favorite Beatle was still prevalent in the ballroom when the Beatle videos were shown! Along with the music videos, the movies were shown, seeing them on the big screen again along with so many others who enjoyed them as much as I did was so fun. Special guests included people who worked for the Beatles and family members. We enjoyed visits with Paul's brother Mike and Louise Harrison, George's sister. Other British Invasion musicians came and performed like Gerry Marsden and Billy J Kramer. I was so excited to hear these songs live I had loved for so long, to get a close look at these people and hear them tell their stories of the time.

After just a few years, Liverpool became the house band. Led by Drew Hill, musician extraordinaire, just seeing the 3 sets of keyboards stacked on top of each other, the guitar around his shoulder and the harmonica on the holder around his neck, he's a one man John Lennon band. Chris on drums has been the steady hand of Ringo style drumming from the start; I know he's going to make the songs sound right. The parts of George and John had been a revolving door until we hit perfection with Glen Burtnik as Paul and John Merjave as George. With the combination of these four talented men, this band is as good as it gets anywhere. Big fun for us as fans was watching them conquer the more complicated songs slowly but surely over the years. Remember, the Beatles never performed live their later creations that were a lot more involved than *She Loves You*. Every year Liverpool presented a new later work, and with perfection! *Strawberry Fields*! Oh wow! *I am the Walrus*! Did you hear that?!! *A Day in the Life*! Did you see Drew pound those keys?!! And then they gave us many of the great songs from their solo careers! I can't praise or thank these guys enough for the top quality performances of this music on such a grand scale!!

I was not able to attend the Fest in the year 2000. When I returned in 2001 there were lots of exciting changes. First, my husband began accompanying me and we met Eddie and began Fest After Hours. Eddie is one of those people who is very friendly and inclusive. He acknowledges and makes everyone he meets feel welcomed. We came across this very talented guitarist leading a late night Beatles sing along. This was a real find and my husband and I quickly joined the many people staying up late singing Beatle songs all night long. As well as a long line of guitars, over the years I have seen people bring bongos, two trombones side by side, a clarinet and endless little percussion instruments. This is a lot going on for three o'clock in the morning and it is great. Eddie told us once they were still singing when the morning delivery of bagels arrived!

One night at about 3 am when we were singing I looked over at the person who had just sat down next to me. It was Donovan! He was our special guest for the weekend performing his iconic songs of the 60's. He has a one of a kind voice and delivery. Hearing *Hurdy Gurdy Man* with Chris from Liverpool accompanying him on sitar is one of my lasting memories. Donovan has graced us with his divine presence at several Fests over the years bringing his spiritual depth which I really appreciate. He gave us a special presentation during the 50th anniversary Fest, truly raising the consciousness in the room.

The Fest Presentation also changed. Gone were the videos in the main ball room. This made sense as we now all had our own copies of the Beatle movies and the videos were all on the internet in YouTube.

This made more time for live music and guest speakers. This worked well. It seemed starting then, each year was better than the next with the top performers that were backed by Liverpool giving us great performances of the British Invasion music. I liked watching the performers realize how beloved they were by us and enjoying themselves with such an enthusiastic crowd response.

Highlights for me included Peter & Gordon who had recently had a small reunion at a charity show to help Mike Smith of the Dave Clark 5 but this was every hit they had! Before the big show, they did an autograph signing which left me feeling concerned about their performance. First person I saw was Gordon who was slumped down in his chair, hat pulled over his eyes, looking rather unshaven and unkempt and scribbling his name without looking at you. Peter was bright eyed, smiling, and talkative. But unfortunately, Gordon was the lead singer! Luckily, to my amazement, I was standing outside the ballroom as the great duo approached for their performance and Gordon had totally transformed. Standing upright, and looking dapper, he was ready for the big night. The stage was set with Liverpool, and musicians lined up all the way across including a guy with a big full sized tuba wrapped around him for the start of *Lady Godiva*. Gordon's voice was as full and deep and enthralling as ever and Peter provided those sweet sounding harmonies. What a thrilling performance! Thank you Fest for Beatle Fans. After Gordon's passing a few years later, Peter returned with his very well presented show highlighting the 60's and his part in it as performer, producer and Record Company executive. It was excellent.

Mark Hudson of the Hudson brothers soon became a yearly guest. Sporting a rainbow colored beard and mustache with an eccentric wardrobe full of purples, Scottish plaids, black everything with studs and topped off with wild berets, Mark brings a personality to match. His performances stir up the performers and the crowd. My favorite is a searing heart felt performance of John Lennon's *Working Class Hero* drawing it out dramatically musically. He really does that anthem justice.

Norman/Hurricane Smith was the Beatles recording engineer through Rubber Soul. He also recorded some hits of his own, most memorable was *Hey Babe, What Would You Say* in the 70's .He visited a Fest at the age of 85, sharing Beatle stories and performing that song for us. A sweet moment was as Norman sang his song, Mark Hudson waltzed his wife from the back of the stage up to him at the microphone. Hurricane passed on within the year so I was so glad we gave him a last chance to perform and Mark gave him and his wife a special moment.

Some of my other favorite moments include Spencer Davis, a quiet unassuming type until he plugs in his electric guitar and starts ripping through *Gimme Some Lovin* and *I'm A Man*. I can imagine him at home with his grandkids...ought oh; grand pa is plugging in his guitar....

We enjoyed Terry Sylvester doing the Hollies Hits, my favorite being *Long Cool Woman in a Black Dress* with Chris from Liverpool banging out that bass drum during the intro of that song and the heartfelt *He Ain't Heavy, He's My Brother*.

One year I looked at the guest list and I told Marianne that I didn't see anyone that special and she replied: "Oh no, Earl Slick is going to be there and he's going to bring down the house!" How did I miss that? And bring down the house he did! All those wild songs from Lennon & Yoko's *Double Fantasy*! The guitar so loud, abrasive and distinctive! Marianne and I were so close we just missed being clunked by the top of the neck of the guitar a few times!

On the stage we have enjoyed music and the tales of the time: Chad & Jeremy who have quite the stage banter as well as their beautiful songs like *Willow Weep for Me* and *A Summers's Song.* Micky Dolenz of the Monkees was full of stories about himself and the Beatles. Hearing the great Monkee hits was a blast to sing and dance to. Peter Noone of Herman's Hermits is as funny as he is talented a musician so we crammed the ballroom to hear his tales of the early days of touring in England and to hear the songs of his we swooned to as kids.

As story tellers go, one of our favorite guests was Victor Spinetti, the well-known Welsh actor who had starring roles in *A Hard Day's Night, Help* and *Magical Mystery Tour.* He coined the term Beatle World, one of music, peace and love. When I arrive at Fest on Friday night, I do not leave the building until Monday, wanting to be in my Beatle World cocoon and truly totally immerse myself in the joy of Beatle world for 3 days. It's ok to let the world as it is slip away for a few days and just feel good.

One of our favorite guest speakers was Patti Boyd. Being George Harrison's first wife, an icon of the 60's herself, as a model and muse for several hit songs, she wrote an autobiography and joined us to promote it. Having saved a Seventeen magazine from back in the day, and drawn a picture of her on her wedding day when I was twelve I had the pleasure of sharing these things with her as she signed my copy of her book.

Marianne stole the show as she showed up in her hand sewn copy of Patti's school girl uniform she wore in her role in *A*

Hard Day's Night, the Beatle movie in which she met George. Patti was quite impressed and pleased!

Marianne has graced the stage at Fest with many costumes of Beatle legend that she has hand sewn for herself. We have Beatle look alike and 60's dress contests during the Beatle Dance Party on Friday evening. Dressed in the very pink outfit that Ahme (Elenor Bron) wears in *Help* was stunning as well as she and I dressing as Julia, John's flamboyant mother, and the prim and proper Aunt Mimi inspired by the movie *Nowhere Boy.* Susan & Judy joined us one year and we dressed as the Beatles in the Alps scene from *Help* complete with Liverpool red and white scarf draped around and connecting us to each other. As coincidence would have it, that year, 4 other women showed up dressed the same! We quickly became *Eight Arms to hold You,* the original title for the movie *Help,* so it always works out. Marianne has also presented herself as Dusty Springfield and most recently Lesley Gore, who because of her double tracked voice, the Beatles told George Martin they wanted to sound like!

One of our more frequent guests has been Lawrence Juber, guitarist for the last line up of Paul McCartney's Wings. Lawrence has mastered the acoustic and electric guitar with a unique style and among the many CD's he has released, two have been of Beatle songs and one of Wings. His presentation of the music on acoustic guitar is complicated and layered expressing special creativity and talent.

We had a very special Fest celebrating 50 years of Beatle music in America and 40 years of Fest. Most special to me was the inclusion of an Ashram to meditate and do yoga with special guest Prudence Farrow. Having had my favorite Beatle song,

Dear Prudence written for her, she spent the most time with the Beatles, especially John & George when they visited the Maharishi in India. With her deep understanding and gifted communication, she shared her spiritual knowledge and the Beatles role in bringing a new and better world to our planet. She said the Beatles were aware of their role and power in the world at that time and consciously chose to be a force of good.

All of this has been brought to us for so many years by the Lapidos family. Originally Mark & Carol and now they are joined by their daughters Jessica & Michele and their friends. They reflect back to us our younger selves with their beautiful colorful clothing and creativity. Thank you so very much.

AFTERWORD

A few weeks back I was shopping at my local health food store and noticed every song I was hearing was the Beatles as a group or solo. As I wheeled my tiny cart down the narrow isles I noticed each employee was singing the songs quietly. When I approached the check out and the woman was singing *Eight Days A Week* I questioned her about the music. She replied that their staff ranged in age from 16 to 83 and The Beatles was the one music they could all agree on and enjoy.

I finish this writing as the world prepares to celebrate John Lennon's 75th birthday. Yoko created another event for peace inviting thousands of people to form a human peace sign in Central Park. They all sang *Imagine* together.

I know that concerts in Liverpool, New York, New Haven, Seattle, California and Philadelphia are planned. I will be attending a live Breakfast With The Beatles with Andre Gardner with my Beatle Family. Peace to all.

DEDICATION TO SID BERNSTEIN BY MARIANNE RUGGERI AND MAUREEN DAYE PIETOSO

Marianne Ruggeri:

For those of us – and that does include most of us – who love the Beatles, have been touched by their message of love, their music, their talent, their wit, their charm, there is one man we must acknowledge for bringing them to the forefront of our attention and to the world's stage.

This visionary noticed very small articles in British newspapers in 1962 about a phenomenon generated by The Beatles. Unprecedented excitement, audiences brought to frenzy, or as it was to be known as Beatlemania. While studying at the new school, part of Sid Bernstein's assignment was to read international newspapers. This was 1962 when there was no internet, no cell phones and no wifi. Newspapers were the source of information in the world.

As a young girl, having a portable television in the kitchen enabled us to watch the evening news during supper. In September 1963, the news just became extended from 15 minutes to 30 minutes. On November 4, 1963, Walter Cronkite was anchoring the evening news. He showed a brief clip of 4 young men playing before Queen Elizabeth at the Royal Command Performance. To introduce their last song of the show, John Lennon spoke into the microphone and said, "Those of you in the cheaper seats, clap your hands. The rest of you rattle your jewelry." They started to sing Twist and Shout.

It was then that I knew something different and very special was going to happen, just like Sid Bernstein could tell by reading the tiny spots in the British papers.

Our generation, the Baby Boomers, define their lives by 2 important events....Where you were when Kennedy got shot (November 22, 1963) and seeing the Beatles on The Ed Sullivan Show on February 9, 1964.

Ed Sullivan had experienced Beatlemania at the airport in Sweden in 1963. He called Sid Bernstein to ask if he should book them on his show. It was Sid who gave the go ahead. A year previously, Sid had already made a deal with Brian Epstein, the Bealtes' manager to play Carnegie Hall on February 12, 1964. He was the man with the foresight, vision and hutzpa to book them into a venue reserved for classical music. He booked them as a "string" quartet! The following year, with the inception of the new baseball stadium for the New York Mets, Sid came up with the idea to book the Beatles to play the new stadium in front of 55,000 fans. This was a first. Performers played theatres and clubs. They didn't play outdoor stadiums in 1965. Today, we take this for granted.

In addition to being a visionary and willing to take chances, Sid Bernstein was down to earth, unassuming, completely interested in people and lived by the code of love for all people. He always had a story to tell and a restaurant or bakery to recommend. His legacy will be forever tied to The Beatles although he promoted numerous top names including The

Rolling Stones and most of the British Invasion Bands, Tony Bennett, Judy Garland and so many more. The Beatles sang and stood for love and equality for all and this is who Sid Bernstein was and is. Thank you, Sid, for picking up the phone to book the Beatles in New York City. That phone call opened up the world stage to the Beatles and started the revolution of an era, never to be matched again.

Sid Bernstein Brought The Beatles To America, But In My Life He Opened Doors...

By Maureen Daye Pietoso

Inexplicably, Sid Bernstein made a tremendous change in my life, before he died last month at age 95. Out of the blue, I came to serve as his publicist for six years and became a dear friend.

When I first met Sid Bernstein at a Fab Faux concert in Pennsylvania in 2004, there was a line of people ahead of me. I wanted to leave Sid alone, and give him some privacy but my friend Geno Barron said he was dear friends with Sid and it was important to say hello. We were near the end of the line, but Sid gave me a signature warm squeeze of my hand, as I shyly said, "Thank you for bringing the Beatles to America." I was thrilled that Geno recommended that I handle publicity for Sid's ventures, and over the moon that the answer was "yes."

Sid presented The Phuket Benefit in 2005 at The Stone Pony in Asbury Park and this was my first event working with him. The show included many of the Jersey Shore regular entertainers, and was headlined by Bobby Bandiera. I wrote an article about the event and it was published on many artists' websites and some internet publications. I have always enjoyed writing feature stories, and Sid piqued my interest for years. He was always involved in multiple projects and events.

I didn't actually become friends with Sid until we got lost for four hours on our way to a party in Rye, New York. Sid shut off my navigator and said he knew how to get there from Manhattan like the back of his hand. Instead of giving direction, we talked. Suddenly, we realized we were on our way to New Jersey rather than Westchester, New York. Sid never lost patience. On the way home from the party, he had us stop at White Castle for burgers and to split a pastry. He always claimed that he was glad that I took a wrong turn because it gave us time to cement our friendship.

I never got to tell Sid that he helped me grow personally and professionally. Prior to meeting Sid, I had struggled with a fear of public speaking. Sid's great confidence and warmth helped me to overcome this. He would talk to me with a mic in a room filled with people, and eventually I became pretty comfortable. My favorite picture of myself and Sid is with him smiling at me, while I'm holding the mic.

Most people like to talk about how Sid loved food, but I think he maintained an even more precious relationship with people. Every day, he called me three or four times. He was verbally demonstrative and expressed that he really believed in me. We could talk about everything, and especially enjoyed discussing our dreams.

Sid even expressed an interest in knowing what artists were my top picks. I made sure that he saw Bruce Springsteen & The E Street Band perform at The Super Bowl on television. "I can see what you see in Bruce," Sid said. "Oh, the showmanship. Honey, we are going to work with him."

Through MySpace and then Facebook, invites poured in for us. Sid was invited to be a dignitary at The NJ Hall of Fame in Newark. We stood on stage with Buddy Valastro, The Cake Boss to present an award. We were also backstage with all sorts of celebrities such as Jack Nicholson, Danny DeVito and Susan Sarandon. Suddenly, Springsteen made a surprise appearance. I told Bruce that Sid Bernstein wanted to meet him. Springsteen quickly responded, "I'll meet Sid."

Imagine my delight at introducing Bruce and Sid. A picture of them made the web site of the NJ Hall of Fame and an article was published about their meeting in Back Streets, the well-known Springsteen fanzine. Though Sid was convinced that we would one day work with Bruce, we never had the time to make it happen.

We had other exciting adventures through the years, and it if pressed to pick one it is this. I knew that Sid was a big fan of The Weavers. He knew that I had been attending the Beacon Sloop Club meetings in Beacon, New York. I offered to introduce Sid to Pete Seeger. Sid said, "set it up." We went. I will never forget introducing Pete Seeger and Sid Bernstein. They are both my heroes. They are humanists in their own ways. Pete is a folk activist, but Sid could always see the most positive traits in any human and promote them to the utmost.

I'm happy that I had an opportunity to once tell Sid that I'm glad that John Lennon had him as a friend because he was very nurturing. Sid said he understood John Lennon.

I feel honored and privileged that my life was touched by Sid's. It meant a great deal to me to attend his funeral recently with my husband Franco Pietoso, who was also a colleague of Sid's, and my dear friend Kaya John, whom I met years ago at The Fest for Beatles Fans.

The funeral was packed with people from all walks of life including famous people. Lenny Kravitz was in the mix outside. He was a little boy when he first knew Sid. I told Lenny how proud Sid was of his career. Lenny gave me a heartfelt hug. We all realized that we have lost a beautiful, uplifting spirit.

Sid changed the world as a famous entertainment promoter. He gave us bands that are iconic and among my top favorites are The Beatles and The Rolling Stones. He gave us an ear that could distinguish white noise from magic. He opened the door for me to be connected in the entertainment industry.

He was a legend, who knew how to make a writer feel. I'll think of him whenever I'm lost, hungry, or daydreaming.